CRAFTING
BEAUTIFUL
JOURNALS &
ALBUMS

CRAFTING BEAUTIFUL JOURNALS & ALBUMS

How to personalize, embellish, and make diaries and scrapbooks

Anna Morgan

NORTH LIGHT BOOKS
Cincinnati, Ohio

A QUARTO BOOK

First published in North America in 2001
by North Light Books,
an imprint of F&W Publications, Inc.,
1507 Dana Avenue
Cincinnati, OH 45207

ISBN 1-58180-135-1

QUAR.TNN

Conceived, designed, and produced by
Quarto Publishing plc
The Old Brewery
6 Blundell Street
London N7 9BH

Senior Project Editor Nicolette Linton
Art Editor Sally Bond
Designer Heather Blagden
Assistant Art Director Penny Cobb
Illustrator Kate Simunek
Photographer Michael Wicks
Text editors Janet Smy, Claire Waite Brown
Index Pamela Ellis

Art Director Moira Clinch
Publisher Piers Spence

Manufactured by Regent Publishing Services
Ltd, Hong Kong
Printed by Leefung-Asco Printers Ltd, China

The author and publisher would like to thank
Sylvie McCracken for designing and making
the variation projects for this book.

Contents

Introduction

Despite the boom of computer technology, books have not lost their appeal. They have an important role to play in our lives, whether they carry the written word or take the form of scrapbooks or folders to store data and documents. The experience of holding a well-loved book is very special and cannot be compared to holding a computer printout or looking at a screen.

ABOVE Collect twigs and leaves, and recycle an old suede jacket to make this soft and supple suede notebook.

Family histories are generally passed down to us through word of mouth, personal journals, scrapbooks and photo albums. We all have a story to tell, whether it be in words, images or as a collection of mementoes. This book shows you how to create and bind your own journals or albums for different occasions and members of the family — and these memories may be treasured as an heirloom by future generations.

Traditional bookbinding is a craft that takes time and patience to perfect, but there are contemporary methods of making and binding books that do not require specialized skills. This book guides you through a variety of simple and more complicated projects with illustrated step-by-step instructions. All the preparation and work can be done on a kitchen table, and needs few specialized tools or equipment.

The book is divided into three sections. The first shows you how to embellish ordinary shop-bought books, albums, organizers, folders, and files with foil, beads, sequins, shells, and pressed flowers.

The second section shows how plain pages can be given a different look. Whether your books are manufactured or handmade, pages can be easily enhanced with simple decorative devices such as deckle edging and liquid embossing. There

are also ideas which demonstrate how loose objects – such as tickets, stamps, postcards, shells, and beads – can be safely contained with the cunning use of elastic, slide index files, envelopes, and collectors' pockets.

The final section shows you how to make books: from the most basic stitched pamphlet to post- and spiral-bound albums and notebooks. More innovative projects, such as the accordion and copper-bound notebooks, are included. A wide selection of materials has been used, including many handmade papers from around the world. Each project captures a different mood: romantic, practical, or sophisticated.

When it comes to making books, there are no absolute rules. So feel free to experiment with your own designs and combine interesting and unusual materials, remembering to choose those of a suitable weight and flexibility. Whether you want to write, paint, or simply store memorabilia, you will find within these pages many different ways of creating a book that is uniquely yours.

LEFT Silver
foil stars and pretty
ribbons are just the
thing to embellish a
special journal.

GETTING STARTED

In this section, we describe and illustrate the different materials and equipment you may need to complete the projects that follow. Many items are common household objects, easy to use even at your kitchen table. Once you've started embellishing and making your own albums, you'll discover exactly how simple and rewarding it can be to produce attractive and innovative presents and keepsafes.

▶ ART CARD STOCK

Thin, stiff art card stock is available from art and office supply stores in a broad range of colors. Suitable for stiff pages but not strong enough for covers, cut art card stock with scissors.

◀ FOAM CORE/POLYBOARD

A layer of foam sandwiched between two layers of card stock, polyboard is used by modelmakers because it is rigid, lightweight, and easily cut with a sharp knife. Punch holes into it with a leather punch, or pierce it with a leather needle. It is a good choice for some types of book cover, although it is only available in black and white.

▲ PLASTIC CARD STOCK

Flexible and durable, this is a fashionable choice for book covers. Available in pretty frosted colors. from large art stores or paper retailers.

Paper and Card Stock

It's important to choose your papers and card stock with care. Think how you'll be using your book — for writing, painting, or as a scrapbook. If you're going to include objects, the paper needs to be up to the job. A photo album needs thin card stock or thick handmade paper to support the photos. And you'll need special paper for painting that won't buckle.

▶ CARDBOARD

This ranges in thickness, quality, and density. Millboard is very hard and dense, and is often used by book-binders to make tough, rigid covers. Available from special suppliers, it needs to be cut with a craft knife with a non-retractable blade — apply pressure when cutting. Pasteboard is of medium density and is available from good art and craft shops, you can also recycle the backs of old sketchbooks and watercolor pads.

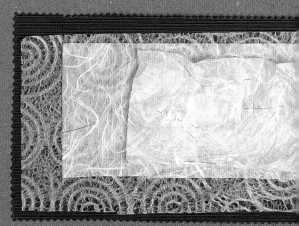

► TRANSLUCENT GLASSINE PAPER Protect your photographs by inserting these between the pages and make sure any papers you use around photographs are acid-free, so they won't eat away at your photos.

▲ COPIER PAPER Ordinary copier paper will suit most book pages. It is inexpensive, easily available, and sturdy enough to withstand wear and tear.

► JAPANESE HANDMADE PAPER Traditionally made, these fine, delicate white tissue papers have intricate lacy patterns and textures. They are expensive, so use them with care. Available from large art stores and art supply catalogs.

◄ DECORATIVE PAPER OR GIFT WRAPPING Available from office supply stores, gift shops — and even recycled from birthday celebrations — these make beautiful end-papers. Make sure they are thick enough, so that the paste doesn't show through.

▲ HANDMADE PAPER The recent revival of handmade papers has resulted in a vast array of colors, textures, and weights of paper made from natural materials — many with decorative additions such as flowers, leaves, and fragrances. Available from art stores and art supply catalogs.

BOOKCLOTH This is a special paper-backed fabric available from specialist suppliers. The paper stiffens the fabric, stops it from fraying, and prevents glue from penetrating.

FABRIC Fabric can be backed with paper or light-weight iron-on interfacing to make it stiffer, stop it from fraying, and prevent paste from seeping through. Choose natural cottons that won't stretch – unless you want a padded cover, when a stretchy fabric may help. Velvet will give a luxurious look, whereas linen looks more organic.

BATTING Terylene batting is available in different thicknesses from fabric and hobby stores.

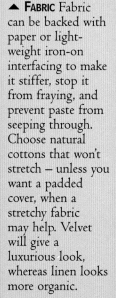

POCKET FILES Buy these in an art and crafts or large office supply store. Used for filing slides, they make excellent pockets.

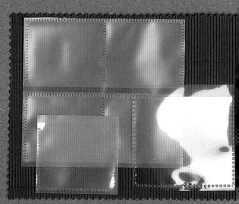

FELT A useful material and a good choice when bookmaking with children. It is easily cut, doesn't fray, can be glued or sewn, and is available from craft stores in a range of attractive colors. It can be used on its own to make a soft cover or as a slipcover.

SEQUINS, BEADS, AND BUTTONS Glue or sew sequins, beads, and buttons onto your cover. You can achieve a fantastic range of effects.

ALUMINUM OR TIN FOIL Emboss motifs into the wrong side of foil with a blunt instrument – such as a stylus or ballpoint pen – to get a relief pattern. Cut out a motif in foil with scissors and attach it to the page using strong double-sided carpet tape.

◀ LACE, RIBBONS, AND EMBROIDERY FLOSS Give your book a rich, tactile quality by stitching or sticking beads, buttons, or sequins to the cover. Lace can be used to decorate the borders of pages or photographs. Weave ribbons together to create a rich and colorful texture.

▲ ENVELOPES You can buy a wide selection of envelopes in all sorts of colors, textures, shapes, and sizes. Attach them to lightweight pages with double-sided tape, and to heavier pages and card stock with double-sided carpet tape.

Embellishments

Choose embellishments that will enhance your book's purpose and add a personal touch. For a lovers' album, use warm and sumptuous materials — ribbon, sequins, and beads all add luxury. Lace adds a lighter, more delicate feel. Objects you've found on your travels — like sea-washed glass or leaves — can be included in your design.

▶ CANDY FOILS Save your candy and chocolate wrappers. Once smoothed out with your finger or an iron, they make vibrant decorations.

▶ PAPER DOILIES Patisserie paper doilies are inexpensive and easily available. Useful for instant decoration, either by gluing sections directly onto the cover or pages, or by using the edges as borders. Spray through the doiley with metallic paint to achieve a lacy effect.

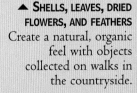

▲ SHELLS, LEAVES, DRIED FLOWERS, AND FEATHERS Create a natural, organic feel with objects collected on walks in the countryside.

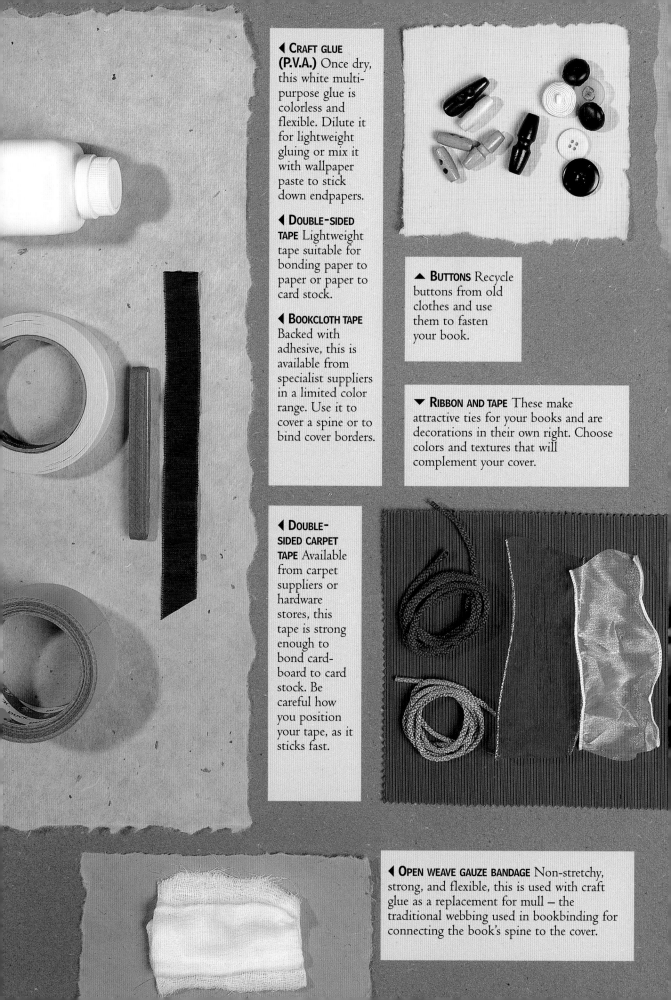

◀ CRAFT GLUE (P.V.A.) Once dry, this white multi-purpose glue is colorless and flexible. Dilute it for lightweight gluing or mix it with wallpaper paste to stick down endpapers.

◀ DOUBLE-SIDED TAPE Lightweight tape suitable for bonding paper to paper or paper to card stock.

◀ BOOKCLOTH TAPE Backed with adhesive, this is available from specialist suppliers in a limited color range. Use it to cover a spine or to bind cover borders.

◀ DOUBLE-SIDED CARPET TAPE Available from carpet suppliers or hardware stores, this tape is strong enough to bond card-board to card stock. Be careful how you position your tape, as it sticks fast.

▲ BUTTONS Recycle buttons from old clothes and use them to fasten your book.

▼ RIBBON AND TAPE These make attractive ties for your books and are decorations in their own right. Choose colors and textures that will complement your cover.

◀ OPEN WEAVE GAUZE BANDAGE Non-stretchy, strong, and flexible, this is used with craft glue as a replacement for mull — the traditional webbing used in bookbinding for connecting the book's spine to the cover.

◀ ORGANIC FASTENINGS Use stones, shells, small pieces of driftwood — whatever you can find — to give your book a truly individual look.

▲ IRON-ON INTERFACING Available in different weights from fabric stores, interfacing is ironed on to stiffen fabric. Two-way iron-on interfacing (like Wonder-Under ®) will bond two fabrics invisibly.

▶ PHOTOGRAPHIC MOUNTING SPRAY This allows you to stick down and even reposition lightweight items such as photographs.

Bindings and fastenings

When deciding on bindings and fastenings, think about how you will use your book. If it's often, make sure the binding is sturdy. If you wish to add or remove pages, plan to use a binding that allows for this. If you're including mementoes, make sure you have a flexible binding, and choose hard covers for a drawing journal.

▶ RAFFIA A simple and natural material, raffia is available in a limited color range. It will give an organic feel to your projects, and can be used to tie together a book or to stitch natural paper pages.

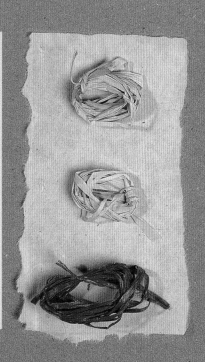

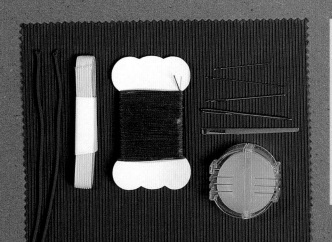

◀ LINEN THREAD AND BEESWAX Linen is a strong, durable thread traditionally used by bookbinders. Run your thread through the beeswax to allow it smooth passage through your pages when stitching.

◀ ELASTIC Thick, round elastic is now sold in exciting colors from office supply and craft stores. Use it to make attractive fasteners for your books or to create a spiral binding.

▶ AWL This pointed metal implement with a wooden handle is useful for making preparatory holes through piles of paper or cardboard. You could improvise with thin knitting needles, darning needles, screwdrivers, or any other sharp-ended tool.

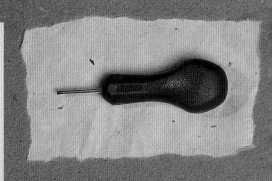

Tools

Many of these projects can be made at your kitchen table with tools you already have at home, like a pencil, ruler, and scissors. There are a few basics you may like to invest in, especially if you take this hobby up long-term. Most arts and crafts stores will stock these pieces, and will be able to give you good advice.

◀ CRAFT KNIFE OR SCALPEL You will need a sharp blade to cut your card stock or paper. Blunt knives tend to pucker and tear the paper, leaving messy edges. A scalpel will cut paper, card stock, polyboard, and thin cardboard. For denser cardboards and millboard, use a non-retractable bladed craft knife.

▶ LEATHER PUNCH A rotating punch, good for making holes in stiff or thick materials. Available at hardware stores.

BONE FOLDER An inexpensive tool made from a smooth lozenge-shaped piece of bone. Available from specialist suppliers, it is used to make folds in paper and card stock, or for smoothing out creases and air bubbles in pasted lining paper. You could improvise with a clean, broad, popsicle stick.

SINGLE HOLE PUNCH Buy this at a stationery suppliers — you'll find it comes in handy when you need to make holes in paper or thin card stock.

STEEL RULER Important for cutting a straight line with a craft knife or scalpel. Remember to hold it down firmly.

SCISSORS Ordinary household scissors can be used for most of the projects in this book. However, you will get an interesting pattern if you use deckle edge scissors. The blades have an interlocking pattern profile on each blade, so that when you cut a piece of card stock or paper, you will get a patterned edge. Choose from a selection of patterns — individually or in combination — to give your pages an attractive fancy edge.

PINKING SHEARS These scissors have zigzag cutting edges to help prevent fabric from fraying when adding decorative detail. You can also use these shears on paper or card stock, but repeated use will blunt them.

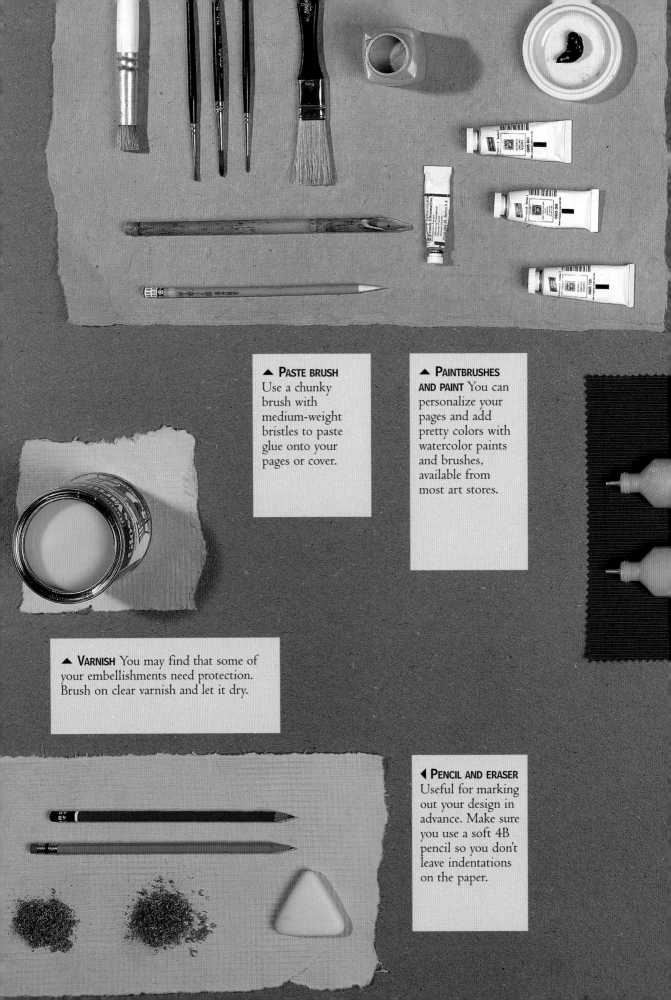

▲ **PASTE BRUSH**
Use a chunky
brush with
medium-weight
bristles to paste
glue onto your
pages or cover.

▲ **PAINTBRUSHES
AND PAINT** You can
personalize your
pages and add
pretty colors with
watercolor paints
and brushes,
available from
most art stores.

▲ **VARNISH** You may find that some of
your embellishments need protection.
Brush on clear varnish and let it dry.

◀ **PENCIL AND ERASER**
Useful for marking
out your design in
advance. Make sure
you use a soft 4B
pencil so you don't
leave indentations
on the paper.

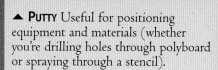

Equipment

As well as acquiring the basic tools, you might like to invest in some equipment to decorate your pages and covers. Most of these can be bought in an arts and crafts store, and over time you can build up a good collection of paints, paintbrushes, pens, pencils, and embossing fluid with which to personalize your albums.

▲ **PUTTY** Useful for positioning equipment and materials (whether you're drilling holes through polyboard or spraying through a stencil).

◀ **EMBOSSING FLUID OR PEN** Available from specialist art and craft suppliers, this fluid — once dry — adds a three-dimensional quality to your page or cover.

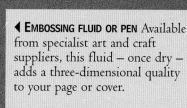

▲ **TELEPHONE DIRECTORIES** These make very useful weights to keep covers flat while they are drying. Any large, heavy book will also work.

▶ **FELT-TIP PENS** Available in a broad range of colors and widths, these are useful for decorating or writing on the pages. Remember not to use these on the back of photos as the colors can bleed through. Use a soft lead pencil instead.

Chapter 1

ON
THE
COVERS

You can use whatever comes to hand to embellish a plain album or folder. All you need is a little imagination and some of the basic materials suggested in the previous section. The following ten projects include clear step-by-step illustrations to give you an idea of the best ways to personalize journals, folders, notebooks, and albums for special occasions and gifts.

Natural notebook

Create your very own rustic book with a delicate dried leaf and a twig found on a country walk. The pages are made from an assortment of handmade papers — you can buy packs of these from good suppliers — and the notebook is bound with raffia to continue the natural theme.

Materials and equipment

- 12x8¼ IN (30x21 CM) SHEET OF HANDMADE PAPER
- CRAFT GLUE (P.V.A.)
- PRESSED OR DRIED LEAF
- ASSORTED SMALL SHEETS OF HANDMADE PAPER
- RAFFIA
- TWIG
- WATERCOLOR PAINTS
- METAL RULER
- SCALPEL
- DARNING NEEDLE
- PAINTBRUSH

CREATE THE BOOK

one Fold the sheet of handmade paper in half and score a fine line down the fold on the outside. Glue the leaf on to the right side of the paper. Leave to dry under a book.

two Cut the smaller handmade paper sheets into decreasing sizes. To achieve a rustic rough edge, make a fold where you want your cutting line to be. Lay the thin edge of the metal ruler along the fold and tear the paper.

RIGHT This charming notebook would make a lovely gift for a friend or you could fill in your own favorite poems and words of wisdom.

three Arrange the pages with the smallest at the center. Score a fine line down the center and fold them in half. Nestle them in the cover.

four Using a needle and raffia, stitch through the center of the pages, about 2½ in (6½ cm) in from the top and bottom. Once through the cover, split each strand of raffia in two.

five Wind the split raffia strands along the twig. Tie the ends at the top and bottom into bows. Using pale watercolors, decorate the front cover and inside pages of the book, leaving each one to dry.

Forget -me-not Visitor's Book

It's very easy to transform a standard visitor's book into one that's unique. Pasting beautiful handmade paper over the covers and decorating them with pressed flowers makes this book one your visitors will certainly never forget.

Materials and equipment

- VISITOR'S BOOK
- 4 TYPES OF HANDMADE PAPER
- CRAFT GLUE (P.V.A.)
- PRESSED FORGET-ME-NOT FLOWERS AND SMALL ROSE LEAVES
- PENCIL
- METAL RULER
- SCALPEL
- BONE FOLDER
- PAINTBRUSH

CREATE THE LOOK

one To make endpapers, open the book and measure the double-page spread. Using a ruler and scalpel, cut two sheets of paper slightly smaller than the open book. Fold the pages in half and paste half of one page to the inside front cover. Smooth out any bubbles with a bone folder, working right into the spine. Leave the second half loose to act as a page. Insert scrap paper to absorb paste and close the book. Place it under a heavy book to dry. Repeat for the back cover.

two Tear a rectangle of handmade paper, slightly smaller than the front cover. Paste it to the cover with craft glue and smooth it with the bone folder. Tear a slightly smaller piece of paper in a different color and paste it on top.

ABOVE What better flower to put on a visitor's book than the forget-me-not?

three Tear strips in contrasting paper and paste these horizontally across the cover. Leave to dry as before. When dry, repeat on the back cover.

four Arrange the pressed flowers along the torn strips. Stick them onto the strips with slightly diluted craft glue. Leave to dry.

five To decorate the back of the book, tear little segments of handmade paper and glue them along the torn strips. Do not use pressed flowers here; they are too fragile and will damage easily.

Garden Notebook

Make a note of where you've planted your bulbs in this practical notebook and keep snippets of information about plant varieties to grow next year. Divided into three sections – flowers, vegetables, and fruits – there's a keepsake envelope attached to the inside front and back covers where you can keep seeds, leaves, or flowers.

Materials and equipment

- SPIRAL BOUND NOTEBOOK WITH COLORED DIVIDERS
- 1/32 IN (1 MM) THICK ALUMINUM OR PEWTER FOIL
- DOUBLE-SIDED CARPET TAPE
- CARD STOCK
- SMALL ENVELOPES
- RULER
- TRACING (TRANSFER) PAPER
- BALLPOINT PEN
- ADHESIVE TAPE
- SCISSORS

CREATE THE LOOK

one Measure your book cover and trace a design from a book or magazine with tracing paper. Cut some aluminum foil to the same size, and place it on a soft cloth or mouse mat. Cover with the tracing, and secure with adhesive tape. Trace over the image with a ballpoint pen, pressing firmly.

two Cover the back of the foil with double-sided carpet tape. Cut out the image using general purpose scissors.

three Choose a design for each divider tab. Trace as for step one and transfer to card stock. Cover the back of the tabs with double-sided tape and cut them out.

ABOVE Transform an ordinary notebook into a special place for your gardening tips and bits. It's very easy to personalize the book with an aluminum plaque and page dividers.

four Cut card stock in the same shape as the tabs, but ⅛ in (3 mm) shorter. Peel the backing off the tape and attach the card to the tab backs, leaving the ends uncovered.

five Divide the book into three equal sections. Place an adhesive tab end on each section, lining up the card with the edge of the page. Press firmly in position. Stick the cover design in place. Stick attractive envelopes to the inside front and back covers.

Fancy File

A ring binder is the basis for this richly decorated and embossed folder. Tissue paper is woven, glued onto the cover, and varnished. Silver foil and embossing paint add the final, sumptuous touches. The inside of the folder is lined with crumpled copper paper.

Materials and equipment

- RING BINDER
- TISSUE PAPER IN 3 COLORS
- DOUBLE-SIDED TAPE
- CRAFT GLUE (P.V.A.)
- SILVER PAPER
- LIQUID EMBOSSING PAINT
- COPPER PAPER
- VARNISH
- RULER
- SCISSORS
- BONE FOLDER
- PAINTBRUSH

CREATE THE LOOK

one Combine three layers of tissue paper, then tear strips at least 1¼ in (3 cm) longer than the folder. Along the inside front and back covers of the folder, place a strip of double-sided tape ⅜ in (1 cm) in from the edge. Remove backing and stick tissue strips in place.

two Starting with the back cover, slip the warp (lengthwise) strips over the top edge and weave the weft (widthwise) strips in place. Paste them down with craft glue as you go, taking care not to spread the paste further than you have woven. Leave to dry then repeat on the front cover.

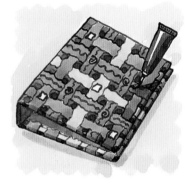

three Once the covers are dry, overlap the remainder of the strips along the spine. Tear bits off to neaten, if necessary. Paste in place and leave to dry.

four Decorate the covers with squares of silver paper, stuck in place with craft glue. Allow each square to dry before adding the next one. Use liquid embossing paint to further embellish your work with lines, crosses, wiggles, and spirals.

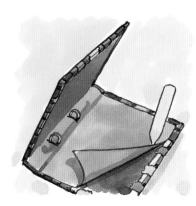

five Measure the inside dimensions of the cover and cut the copper paper ¾ in (2 cm) smaller. Cut slots in the paper to accommodate the ring binders. Paste the paper in place. Smooth with a bone folder. Place heavy books on each side and leave to dry. Coat your fancy folder with several layers of varnish for protection.

ABOVE Transform a plain ring binder into an exciting new folder with a collage of tissue and embossing paints.

E-mail File

Store your e-mail correspondence — whether it's on floppy disk or on paper — in this innovative plastic file. Round elastic has been threaded onto the front of the folder, creating a secure place to store disks. To personalize this project, include your favorite pictures in the special picture frames and on the disk holder.

Materials and equipment

- FLOPPY DISK CASE
- PLASTIC EXPANDING FILE FOLDER
- SNAP FASTENER
- TRANSLUCENT PAPER
- ROUND ELASTIC
- RULER
- CRAFT KNIFE
- CUTTING MAT
- HOLE PUNCH
- AWL
- MALLET

CREATE THE LOOK

one Take the floppy disk case and mark out a 4 in (10 cm) square for a picture frame. Cut out the square with a craft knife for your photograph.

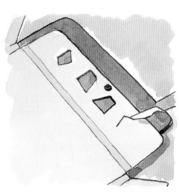

two Put the plastic expanding file folder on a cutting mat, and cut out four picture frames down the front flap with a craft knife. Insert a snap fastener halfway down the opening to secure the file.

three Take a piece of translucent paper and cut a strip for the back of the picture frames. Punch holes for the elastic at 2 in (5 cm) intervals.

four Using the strip as a template, mark out and punch corresponding holes on the plastic holder. Knot together with elastic.

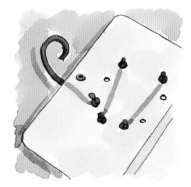

five Turn the folder over. With an awl and hammer, make holes for the elastic to attach the floppy disk case to the front cover. Thread elastic through the holes.

SIX Insert photographs in the frames. Design and print out computer graphics on paper for the inside pages, to match the overall look of your e-mail file.

A B O V E Make a cutting-edge e-mail file with the technology you use each and every day. Inside the file, there are small picture frames to house photographs of your friends and loved ones.

Vacation Journal

Do you keep a journal of your memories while on vacation? Here's a way to decorate the cover with a collage made from some of your mementoes: why not use a thin piece of wood as the base on which to stick your finds and attach an envelope to store your treasures.

Materials and equipment

- SPIRAL BOUND NOTEBOOK
- RAFFIA
- TISSUE OR FINE PAPER IN CONTRASTING COLORS
- SPRAY ADHESIVE
- CRAFT GLUE (P.V.A.)
- SMALL ENVELOPE
- RIBBON
- PIECE OF THIN WOOD, SMALLER THAN NOTEBOOK
- SAND, SHELLS, AND STARFISH
- STRONG GLUE (TWO PART EPOXY)
- PENCIL
- HOLE PUNCH
- SCISSORS

CREATE THE LOOK

one Tear out a page from your notebook and use the holes to mark out spaces around the edge of the front and back covers.

two Using a punch, make holes all the way round the two covers.

three Tie a knot in the end of a length of raffia. Thread from the inside corner next to the spine and oversew all round the cover edges, including the spine edge. Secure with a knot on the inside when complete.

four Tear the fine colored paper into small pieces. Stick it to the inside cover and endpages with spray adhesive.

ABOVE Inside the book covers, there are two handy places to keep loose items such as tickets, photos, shells, and postcards. Tuck larger ones inside the ribbon cross. Smaller ones can be stored in the envelope.

six Make a cross on the inside cover for your keepsakes: tie a knot in a length of raffia or ribbon. Thread through from the outside corner hole across the inside and out at the diagonal. Tie a knot on the outside and trim. Repeat on the opposite edge.

eight Form a collage with shells or other memorabilia and attach them using craft glue.

five Use craft glue to fix a small envelope to the center of the endpage for your treasured items.

seven Spray adhesive over the piece of wood. Sprinkle over sand.

nine Mark out the position for the collage on the front cover of your notebook. Apply strong glue to the underside of the collage and press it firmly in place, taking care not to break fragile items.

ten Cut a length of ribbon long enough to tie around the book. Secure it with a knot around the central ring of the binding and tie it with a bow.

RIGHT Collect mementoes from your holiday to make a lovely cover for your journal. Shells, starfish, and sand have been glued to a plaque and fixed on the front, and a ribbon keeps the whole thing secure.

Mosaic Album

Keep any beautiful candy wrappers you come across — smoothed out they make exquisite decorations. Here, a recess has been cut in which the foils are laid. Several layers of waterproof varnish protects the foils and gives them a jewel-like quality. The endpapers have been decorated with inks and snippets of confetti-like foil to complement the cover.

Materials and equipment

- ARTIST'S DRAWING BOOK
- COLORED CANDY WRAPPERS
- DOUBLE-SIDED TAPE
- WATER SOLUBLE VARNISH
- COLORED ELASTIC CORD
- 4 SEQUINS
- INKS AND PENCIL
- RULER
- SCALPEL
- SCISSORS
- PAINTBRUSHES

CREATE THE LOOK

one Decide how much of your book you want to decorate and rough out your design on paper. Mark out the area on the book to be used. Using a scalpel, score a recess ½ in (1 mm) into the cover along your markings.

three Smooth out your foil wrappers, using your finger or a flat implement. Stick double-sided tape to the wrong side of each piece you intend to use.

two Using the tip of your scalpel, ease out the first corner. You should then be able to pull off this layer.

four Cut your planned shapes out of the foil wrappers and remove the tape backing as required.

RIGHT To create a rose petal window, cut a rectangle right through the cover with a scalpel. Cut two pieces of acetate ³/8 in (1 cm) larger than the window. Sandwich handmade paper rose petals between the sheets and stick the acetate together with craft glue. Stick this to the inside front cover and hide the window edge with gold thread.

VARIATION

five Stick the foils into the recess. Either layer your background colors first, then add other pieces, or fit the shapes together like a jigsaw.

six Apply several coats of water soluble varnish (solvent-based varnish may take the color off the foil). Leave each coat to dry before applying the next.

seven Stick down colored elastic cord the width of your recess. Glue a sequin onto each corner.

eight Paint the endpapers with inks. Choose colors that fit your scheme. If you want a really rich color, apply several layers of ink, letting each coat dry between applications.

ABOVE Squares of foil are scattered over the painted endpapers and then varnished for protection.

RIGHT Candy wrappers make fabulous decorating materials as they come in such sumptuous colors. Create a design with them to decorate the front of your book.

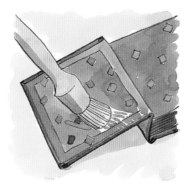

nine Snip more foil to decorate the endpages. Remove the tape backing and position as desired.

ten Apply varnish to the decorated endpages to protect them.

Wedding Album

Layers of delicate organza and Indian mirror decorations transform a plain wedding album bought from a stationer's into a precious memento of a special day. To close the album, thread a ribbon through a slot in the spine and tie it in a bow.

Materials and equipment

- WEDDING OR PHOTO ALBUM (HERE WITH A SILVER COVER)

- 5 ORGANZA PIECES IN DIFFERENT COLORS

- CRAFT GLUE (P.V.A.).

- 1/2 IN (1 1/2CM) WIDE RIBBON ABOUT 24 IN (61 CM) LONG

- INDIAN MIRROR DECORATIONS, SEQUINS, BEADS, OR FLAT-BACKED BUTTONS

- SMALL ENVELOPE

- DOUBLE-SIDED CARPET TAPE

- RULER

- SCISSORS

- SCALPEL

- BONE FOLDER

CREATE THE LOOK

one Measure the cover of the book and cut three pieces of organza to fit, each in a slightly smaller size.

two Fray the ends of each piece by pulling away the cross-threads of the cloth.

three Spread a thin coat of craft glue over the cover of the book. Lay on the largest piece of organza and smooth out. Repeat with the other two sheets of organza. Leave to dry.

four On the inside cover, use a scalpel to cut a lengthways slot mid-way along the spine fold, at least as wide as the ribbon. Cut only through the cover and not into the stitching. Repeat at the back.

five Thread the ribbon from the inside front cover over the outside spine and in through the back. You need enough to wrap around your book once and tie with a generous bow.

six Using craft glue, stick the ribbon to the inside front cover. When dry, repeat at the back.

seven Open the book and cut two organza rectangles to fit across the width of the inside front and back pages and covers. These will be the endpapers.

RIGHT Fine organza has been pasted down to make sumptuous endpapers and a silver envelope is added to keep small mementoes safe.

eight Glue the first piece of organza onto the inside back cover only, allowing enough give to enable the book to open or close. Press along the spine fold with a bone folder and smooth out any creases. Leave to dry. Repeat on inside front cover.

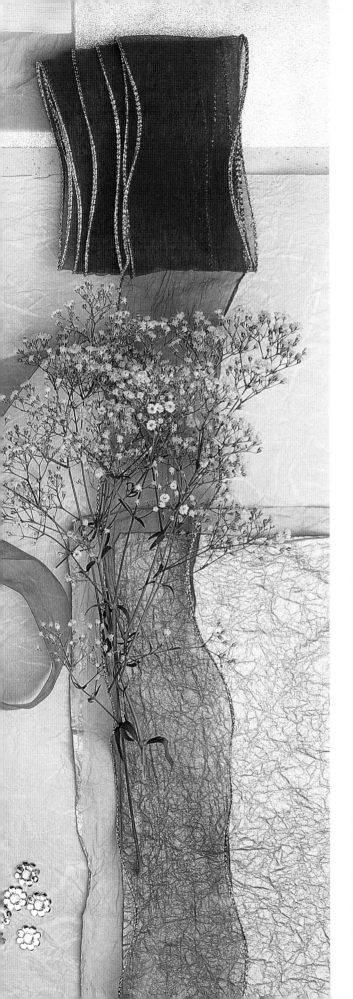

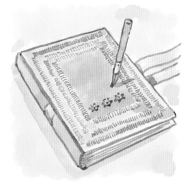

nine Glue decorations in place on the front cover with craft glue. Leave to dry.

ten Attach an attractive envelope to the inside front page with double-sided carpet tape.

LEFT Three layers of floaty organza, Indian beaded mirrors, and a pretty ribbon decorate this store-bought album. Perfect for your own special day, or as a personalized gift for friends.

Beaded Diary

This bead-encrusted diary with its ribbon tie and lavish lining paper is the perfect place to write down your personal thoughts. The polymer clay lattice work was built up on a plain art book, and beads and fake gems laid down for decoration.

Materials and equipment

- ART BOOK OR DIARY
- RIBBON
- SMALL HANDFUL OF POLYMER CLAY, ROLLED OUT TO 1/4 IN (6 MM)
- STRONG GLUE (TWO PART EPOXY)
- CRAFT GLUE (P.V.A.)
- BEADS IN VARIOUS COLORS
- 10 SMALL GREEN GEMS AND 8 RED PASTE GEMS
- PRETTY ENDPAPERS
- RIBBON
- SCALPEL
- ROLLING PIN AND BOARD
- CUTTING SURFACE
- BONE FOLDER
- PENCIL AND METAL RULER

CREATE THE LOOK

one With the scalpel, make a slit midway along the front and back cover wide enough to fit your ribbon. Make the cut as close into the spine as possible without cutting any stitches.

two Roll out the polymer clay with a rolling pin to 1/4 in (6 mm) thickness. Using a scalpel, ruler, and cutting mat, cut thin strips to make a border for your beadwork.

three Using a pencil, draw the border and lattice pattern on the front cover. Use strong glue to fix the polymer clay border in position. Roll the remaining clay more thinly and cut finer strips. Glue the strips in place for the lattice. Working in a well-ventilated room, bake the clay in the oven. This can be for less than the recommended time on the packaging, since the strips are very thin.

four While the clay is baking, plan your bead color scheme. When the clay is cooked and firm, leave to cool. Spread a layer of craft glue on the bottom of each section. Fill with beads and leave to dry.

five Glue the small gem stones onto the latticework, perhaps with tweezers. Place red ones on the outside and green on the inside.

seven Cut your ribbon long enough to tie around your book – including a bow. Thread the ribbon through from the inside cover, around the spine and through the back cover slit.

eight Measure your book when its open and cut endpapers to fit. Paste one sheet to the inside cover, over the ribbon, smoothing it in with a bone folder. Work the paper right into the spine's groove. Close and leave to dry, with a loose sheet of paper in between to absorb surplus glue. Place a light weight on top – do not crush your art work. When dry, repeat for the back cover.

six Use craft glue to stick the remaining beads around the edge of the book cover,

BELOW Rich gold endpapers add to the luxurious look of this beaded diary. Here, the ribbon was threaded around the book after the endpapers were glued down, to show off the colorful ribbon.

VARIATION

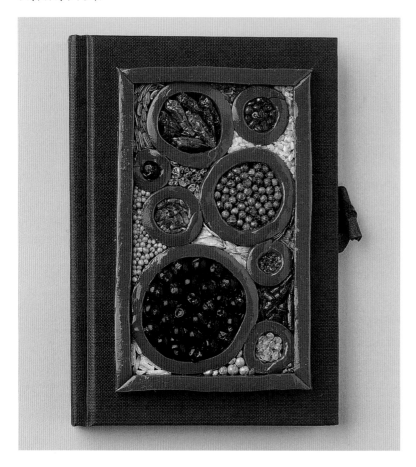

ABOVE To add a touch of spice to your diary, raid your kitchen cabinets. Fill the spaces between the clay with craft glue and drop in a variety of different dried seeds and spices. Cover with a coat of clear varnish to protect and hold the seeds and spices in place.

one Roll out the polymer clay with a rolling pin to ¼ in (6 mm) thickness. Using a scalpel, ruler, and cutting mat, cut thin strips and form them into circles to match your design. Use strong glue to fix the clay into place and bake as before.

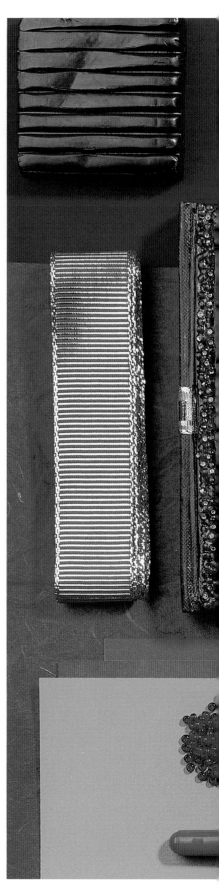

RIGHT Beaded and bejeweled, this is a beautiful and unusual cover to make for a diary — for yourself or as a precious gift for a special friend.

Linen Organizer

It's not difficult to give your personal organizer a new look — just cover it with fabric. Here an old black and white family photo, transferred onto white cotton, forms the centerpiece. The cover is made from natural linen with a blanket stitched border. Inside, two pretty pockets have been created to store your keepsakes.

Materials and equipment

- PERSONAL ORGANIZER
- THIN FOAM
- LINEN AND RIBBON
- SEWING THREAD, NEEDLE AND PINS
- BIAS TAPE
- 2 BUTTONS
- FABRIC PHOTO (TRANSFER PHOTO ONTO FABRIC AT A PHOTOCOPY OR PRINT STORE.)
- DOUBLE-SIDED CARPET TAPE
- SCISSORS
- IRON

CREATE THE LOOK

one Cut any snap fasteners off the covers. Stick two sheets of foam sized ½ in (1¼ cm) smaller than your personal organizer onto its front and back.

two Cut the linen 1½ in (4 cm) wider than the organizer and long enough to wrap around the inside of the covers to create pockets.

VARIATION

BELOW You can buy different types of paper to fit personal organizers — choose them to suit the color and style of your cover.

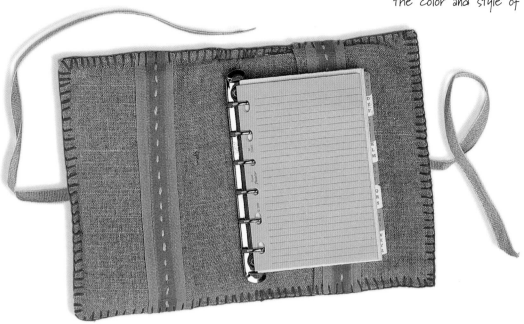

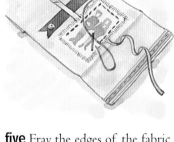

three Turn the two short ends back and iron flat, remembering to tuck under the edge for a hem. Turn over ⅜ in (1 cm) at the top and bottom. Pin two strips of ribbon in place along the edges. Stitch in place with running stitch, securing the hem on the underside.

four Sew a piece of bias tape vertically in the middle of the linen piece, adding two buttons to make the spine. Then cut a length of tape long enough to wrap round the file and tie into a bow. Sew this to what will be the middle of the back of the outside cover.

five Fray the edges of the fabric photo transfer. Stitch it into position over the ribbon as the centerpiece of the front cover.

LEFT To create a different look for your organizer, use velvet to cover it. Arrange a slip of lace and a dry leaf between laminating sheets. Position over the book cover and punch holes in each corner with a hole punch. Secure the sheets onto the velvet with glass beads large enough to obscure the holes.

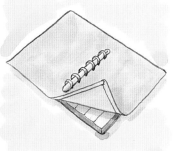

six Cut out a piece of linen large enough to line your organizer with a ¾ in (2 cm) border. Cut a slot from the center of the fabric the same shape as the ringbinder, but slightly smaller. Iron back a ³/₈ in (1 cm) hem all round.

seven Iron the lining in place, stretching it over the ringbinder and sliding the edges under. Hold in place with double-sided carpet tape.

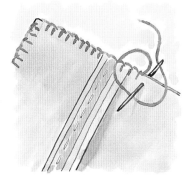

eight Iron a ⅜ in (1 cm) hem all the way around the cover fabric. Place a ¾ in (2 cm) strip of double-sided carpet tape along the outside spine to secure the cover. Pin the cover in place and use blanket stitch all around the edge with the sewing thread.

LEFT Personalize your organizer with a favorite photograph or picture. Your local photocopy or print store can transfer it for you. Stitch the cloth onto the front as decoration. Choose thread and fabric ties to complement your picture.

Chapter 2

BETWEEN THE COVERS

Don't judge a book by its cover alone. The insides can be just as attractive, and can even be used for storing mementoes. In this section you will learn how to make your own paper from natural and recycled materials, to decorate and embellish pages with different techniques — such as deckle edging and embossing — and to make envelopes and pockets in which to store your treasures.

Materials and equipment

- NEWSPAPER — to protect work surfaces and help dry sheets

- WASTEPAPER — you can recycle most papers, but not newsprint

- WATER

- SPONGE

- BLENDER OR LIQUIDIZER — this must include a circuit breaker

- VAT — bigger than your largest mold

- FELTS — buy man-made felts or use striped viscose dishcloths (these should be twice as long as the mold and a little wider)

- MOLD — stretch plain screen mesh over a rectangular frame

- SIEVE

- DRIED SEEDS, GRASSES, FLOWERS, LEAVES

- TWEEZERS

- CAPILLARY MATTING — available from garden centers

- PRESS — a pair of melamine-faced plywood boards and four G-clamps

- IRON

- PALETTE KNIFE (OPTIONAL)

- CLOTHES LINE OR FOLDING CLOTHES RACK AND PEGS (OPTIONAL)

- BROWN PAPER (OPTIONAL)

MAKING PAPER

Customize your books with handmade paper using materials collected from your own backyard or on any country walk. It's easy to create papers with fresh and pressed flowers, petals, seeds, grasses, and leaves. Making paper can be a messy business, so keep your work space as tidy as possible and cover any surfaces with water absorbers, such as newspaper or old towels.

PREPARING RECYCLED PULP

1 Soak 18 sheets of 8½ x 11 in (A4) wastepaper – not newsprint – in 1 gallon (4½ liters) of water in a vat overnight.

2 Tear the paper into small pieces. Fill a 1 quart (1.2 liter) kitchen blender jar ¾ full and add batches of paper (about ⅙ at a time). Blend to a smooth pulp.

Bulrush

Ideal for endpapers, this smooth textured paper is made from bulrush (also known as brown busbies, reed mace or cattail), which commonly grows wild in ditches and at the edges of ponds and lakes. Bulrushes can be grown at home, but be careful they don't dominate your other plants.

one Harvest the seeds by putting the rusty-brown flower spikes into a brown paper bag. Break apart the spikes in the bag, releasing the seeds. Store them in a dry place.

two Add the seeds to prepared paper pulp and mix lightly to distribute them.

three Form sheets and couch them as usual. Press and hang the sheets to dry.

SHEET FORMING

3 Pour the pulp into a vat and repeat the process until the vat is ¾ full. Add water if necessary.

1 Dampen 13 felts. Fold one into a small couching pad. Place the pad under one half of another felt.

2 Stir the pulp thoroughly and let the waves subside.

Corn on the cob

Paper made with silk from maize or a corn cob has a fine texture, which makes it good to write on. Once you've removed the silks from the maize or corn, cook the cobs for a delicious snack.

one Take the silks from the cob when it is mature. Dry in an airy place and store in a dry bag.

two Cut the silks into small pieces and blend lightly into the prepared pulp.

three Form sheets and couch them as usual. Press and hang the sheets to dry.

SHEET FORMING CONTINUED

3 Lower the mold vertically into the vat on the side furthest away from you. Tilt the top end downward. Pull it toward you until it is horizontal below the surface of the pulp.

4 Hold the mold horizontally and raise it out of the vat. Water will drain back into the vat.

5 If there is any unevenness on the sheet, turn the mold over and let the pulp drop back into the vat. Stir and scoop again until you have an even covering of pulp.

Potpourri

Depending on the flowers and leaves you use, potpourri can give your paper an individual tint. Lavender and rose petals work especially well.

one Grind up seeds or spices in a coffee grinder. Crush the pot-pourri to make the pieces smaller.

two Add the potpourri to the prepared pulp and blend it in lightly.

three Form sheets and couch them as usual. Press and hang the sheets to dry.

COUCHING

1 Hold the mold over the vat to drain. Position the mold over the couching pad. Turn the mold over onto the couching pad and press down.

2 Press a damp sponge onto the net to remove water. To loosen the sheet before lifting up the mold, rock the mold from side to side. Fold the other half of the felt over the sheet. Lay a fresh felt on top and start to couch your second sheet.

STORING PULP

Sieve the excess pulp and leave it to dry. Keep in an airtight container in a refrigerator for not longer than a week (longer in a freezer).

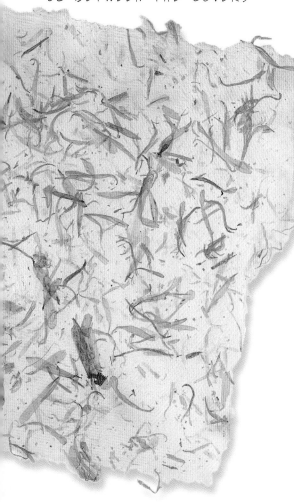

Marigold

Marigold petals come up beautifully in handmade paper, retaining their vibrant yellow color.

one Collect marigold flower heads and remove the petals. Press the best petals between sheets of absorbent paper to dry. Dry the remaining petals.

two Stir the unpressed petals onto the prepared pulp.

three Form a sheet and couch it. Position the pressed petals onto the sheet with tweezers. Press, then hang the sheet to dry.

ADDING DRIED PLANT MATERIAL

If you wish to add dried plant material, use tweezers to place it on each sheet after couching.

PRESSING

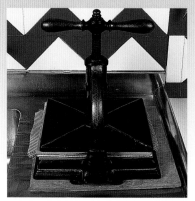

Cut two pieces of capillary matting a little larger than the felts. Place the matting at the base and top of the pile of sheets and felts. Put these between the boards of a press and tighten until no water comes out.

DRYING OPTIONS

1 NEWSPAPER DRYING – Once pressed, build a post of six sheets of newspaper, one felt-and-sheet sandwich, six sheets of newspaper, and so on. Leave for several hours. Repeat if necessary until dry.

Embossing

To make a patterned imprint on a sheet of paper, use anything with a raised pattern, for example a leaf.

one Form a sheet of paper and couch it.

two Place a strongly patterned leaf on the surface of the sheet. Fold over the felt, press, and dry the sheet between some newspaper.

three When the sheet is dry, lift off the leaf with tweezers.

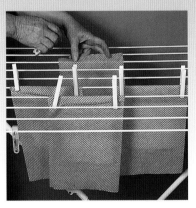

2 AIR DRYING – Do not press. Instead, let your sheet drain flat in the mold until it is only damp. Lean it at an angle on dry newspaper in a dark airy place. When the sheet is dry, use a palette knife to work the paper off the mold.

3 HANGING – Once pressed, hang the felt-and-sheet sandwich on a washing line or drying rack. Secure with clothes pegs at the edges.

4 IRONING – Once pressed, sandwich the sheets individually between brown paper and use a moderate heat, keeping the iron moving until the sheet is dry.

Deckle Edging

Deckle edge scissors have a variety of attractive cutting edges and this is a simple way to add interest to an album. When first using the scissors, be careful to keep the pattern consistent. Your finished work will look best if the corners are symmetrical (you can even buy special corner scissors and punches for this).

Materials and equipment

- POST BOUND ALBUM
- SHEETS OF CONTRASTING PAPER
- STAR STAMP
- FOIL
- CRAFT GLUE (P.V.A.)
- DOUBLE-SIDED CARPET TAPE
- DECKLE EDGE SCISSORS
- PENCIL
- CRAFT KNIFE
- BONE FOLDER
- HOLE PUNCH
- SCISSORS

DECORATING PAPER

You can turn plain paper into exciting and interesting pages by employing simple decorative devices such as using deckle edge scissors, embossing liquids, and lace. Use these techniques to jazz up a ready-made book or add extra interest to one that you have made yourself.

CREATE THE LOOK

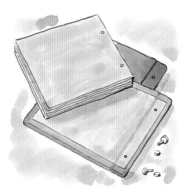

one Disassemble the book so that you have loose pages to work with.

two Cut two sheets of contrasting paper to line the cover and two to make the endpapers. Using the deckle edge scissors, cut a fancy border about ¼ in (6 mm) from the edge around three sides of all the loose pages.

RIGHT
Choose pretty pastel papers in diminshing sizes and cut the edges with deckle edge scissors. Stack them and tie them into your album with a delicate ribbon.

VARIATION

three Stamp out stars randomly, but evenly spaced, all over two of the sheets. On the other two sheets, draw a larger star in a central position. Cut out all the stars with a craft knife.

ABOVE Make a book for a friend to record her new baby's first year. Deckle edged card stock or paper can make a decorative border around a photograph. This is stuck onto the cover of the album and texture is added with embossing liquid.

four Line each sheet with enough foil to cover the stars. Paste the sheet in position with craft glue. Carefully smooth out any crinkles with a bone folder.

five Punch holes, to line up with the other pages, in the margin of the single star sheets.

six Paste the multi-star pages into position on the front and back cover. Leave to dry under a heavy book or telephone directory. If the paper does not take paste well, use double-sided tape.

seven Using the contrasting paper, cut a strip as wide as the deckle edged margin and back it with double-sided tape. Then trim a smaller strip with a deckled border. Punch holes with an awl to line up with the posts and stick the strip in place along the margin on the inside front cover.

eight Thread all the pages in position, with the single star sheets acting as endpapers at the front and back of the book. Screw the front cover back onto the posts.

RIGHT This pretty pink velvet covered album originally had fairly dull endpapers. A contrasting color to the cover was chosen instead and pepped up with cut-out silver foil stars.

Embossed Album

Embellishing with embossing liquid is easy, although it requires patience and a steady hand. To gain confidence, draw out your pattern and pipe over the lines, progressing to working freehand. Embossing liquid responds best to a continuous flowing movement, so maintain an even pressure, rather than stopping and starting. The liquid smudges easily, so let each area of pattern dry.

Materials and equipment

- POST BOUND ALBUM
- SHEET OF CARD STOCK
- EMBOSSING LIQUID IN PEARLIZED SILVER, PINK, GREEN, AND MAUVE
- PENCIL
- SCISSORS
- CRAFT KNIFE
- DECKLE EDGE SCISSORS

CREATE THE LOOK

one Make a heart template by folding a sheet of card stock in half and drawing the shape before cutting. Unscrew the album and remove a page. Draw round the heart shape onto the page.

two Pierce the center of the heart with a craft knife. Insert the deckle edge scissors through the hole and snip about 1 in (2½ cm) in from the edge to get a pretty border.

three Pipe a ¼ in (6 mm) line around the heart with the pearlized silver embossing liquid. Leave to dry. Using the same liquid, make a scalloped edge along this line and then add dots to each scallop. Leave to dry.

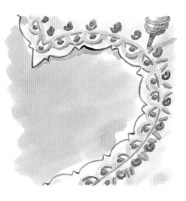

four To create a rosebud effect, make a small spiral with the pearlized pink fluid at every scallop interval. Leave to dry before piping in the pearlized green leaves.

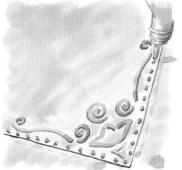

ABOVE Cut the card stock with deckle edge scissors to make a romantic mount for your special photograph. Decorate it with piped patterns using embossing liquid.

five Decorate each corner with groups of three rosebuds, stylized leaves, and silver corner tabs. Leave to dry.

six Add broad scrolls in each corner. Finish by adding a dotted border of delicate pearlized mauve dots.

VARIATION

one To create a picture frame, measure the size of the picture you wish to frame. Decide on the depth of frame and draw both inner and outer lines with a ruler and pencil. The distance between the lines should be about 1 in (2½ cm). Cut the frame out along the pencil line using deckle edge scissors along the pencil line. To create a decorative inner edge, pierce the center of the paper using a scalpel, and cut along the pencil line with a different pair of deckle blades.

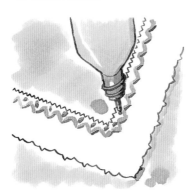

two Using pearlized mauve embossing liquid, pipe a border pattern around the inner frame. Allow to dry. Add silver dots between the scallops.

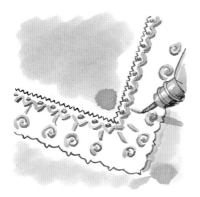

three Add stylized rosebuds along the outer edge and leave to dry. Join the rosebuds to the inner edge with pearlized green stems. Leave to dry.

four All around the border add pearlized silver crosses between each rosebud. Position the photograph in the frame and stick in place with photo corners. Return the page to the album and tighten the screws.

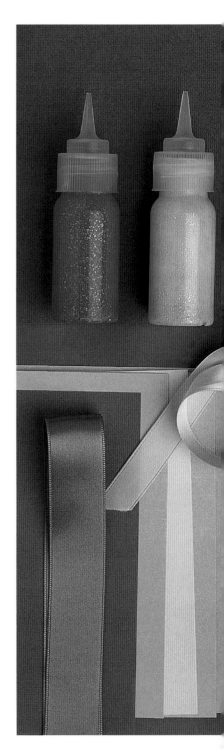

RIGHT Use embossing liquid to embellish your paper. With practice, you can make some fantastic, colorful patterns.

ABOVE Create tailor-made photographic mounts in the shape and color of your choice. Here, a cherished photograph is enhanced by deckle edging and embossing, two simple techniques that will add an individual touch. Practice first on a piece of paper, so that you can avoid any messy errors.

Lacy Album

Lace edging makes a charming addition to an album, particularly if it contains old family pictures. Using lace on every page would make the album too bulky, so continue the theme by spraying some pages with silver paint through paper doilies.

Materials and equipment

- SPIRAL BOUND ALBUM
- NEWSPAPER
- PAPER DOILIES
- SPECIALIST PAPERS, JAPANESE WHITE HANDMADE COVER PAPER; LACY HANDMADE PAPER; FILMY-TEXTURED PAPER
- CAN OF SILVER SPRAY PAINT
- CRAFT GLUE (P.V.A.)
- EMBOSSING LIQUID IN PEARLIZED SILVER
- RIBBON AND LACE TRIMMINGS
- LACE-TRIMMED OLD HANDKERCHIEF
- FABRIC GLUE AND FACE MASK
- SCISSORS AND BONE FOLDER
- REUSABLE STICKY PUTTY

CREATE THE LOOK

one Protect your work surface with newspaper. Scatter paper doilies randomly over the cover paper and album pages. Hold the doilies in position with putty. Wearing a mask, spray silver as directed on the tin.

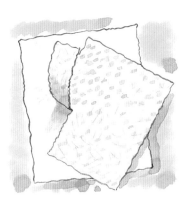

two Cut and tear lacy handmade paper into strips. Arrange in a pleasing way before pasting.

three Paste the silver sprayed paper into position covering just over half the bottom of the book. Then paste the soft, filmy-textured paper at the top of the book.

four Paste a strip of lacy scalloped paper over the edges of the other two papers. Smooth into position using a bone folder. Leave under a heavy book or telephone directory to dry.

RIGHT Lace can be used to frame a special photograph. It is particularly poignant if the lace has an association with the person in the photograph.

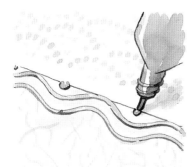

five Using pearlized silver embossing liquid, draw a double wavy line along the seam of the papers. Make dots inside each wave and leave to dry.

six Continue to embellish the book with scrolls along alternate half sides and make a dotted border along the other half sides. Repeat at the top and bottom.

seven Knot a ribbon midway onto the spiral binding. It should be long enough to wrap around the book and tie with a generous bow.

VARIATION

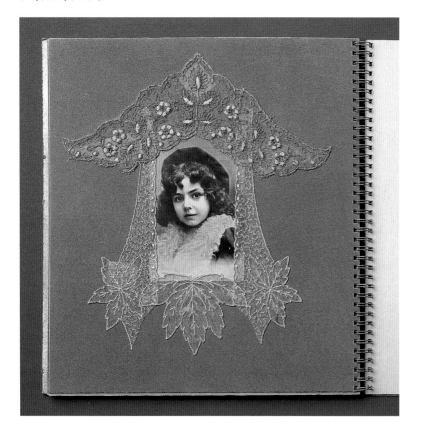

LEFT Find unusual shapes in lace and you can make spectacular collages with old pictures. Use fabric glue to stick the lace to your paper and watch your image take shape.

MORE LACE

Paste a lacy handkerchief onto the page with fabric glue. Mount the photograph on the fabric.

Use lace trimming as a border for your photograph. Just cut the pieces to fit the four sides, and paste it on with fabric glue.

Personalize the pages with hand-painted labels. Use watercolor paint to complement the album and photograph, and stick it onto the page with craft glue.

RIGHT This spiral bound pastel drawing book forms the basis for a lovely photographic album. The cover has had various Japanese handmade papers pasted onto the front and silver paint has been sprayed through paper doilies to give a lacy effect.

Finders keepers

The stylish plastic paper cover of this album frames a 3D object and the richly decorated inside pages allow you to keep collected items such as beads, shells, or glass fragments safely.

Materials and equipment

- SHEET OF PLASTIC PAPER 11 1/2x25 IN (29x63 CM)

- 10 SHEETS OF CARD STOCK 10 1/2x13 3/4 IN (27x35 CM)

- KETTLE DESCALER

- POLYBOARD

- CRAFT GLUE (P.V.A.)

- SCRAPS OF FABRIC OR PAPER

- 2 SHEETS OF PAPER

- EMBOSSING LIQUID IN PEARLIZED MAUVE, GREEN, AND PINK

- EPOXY GLUE

- ELASTIC

- CRAFT KNIFE AND METAL RULER

- BONE FOLDER

- HOLE AND LEATHER PUNCHES

- HAMMER AND NAIL

- BLOCK OF SCRAP WOOD

ADDITIONS & INSERTIONS

Often the keepsakes we put in our books or albums – such as leaves, shells, seeds, letters, and cards – are not flat and easy to stick down. The solution is to create pockets, envelopes, noteboards, and frames that will store them in beautiful and original ways.

CREATE THE BOOK

one To form the book's spine, lightly score two vertical parallel lines 2 in (5 cm) apart down the center of the plastic paper using a metal ruler and craft knife. Carefully fold the plastic along these lines.

two Score a 2 in (5cm) margin down the short side of each sheet of card. Fold this margin over, smoothing it into place with a bone folder. This will act as the page spacer.

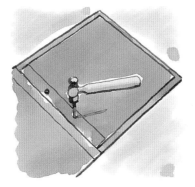

three Punch holes about 6 in (15 cm) apart in the margins of all the sheets of card stock.

four Position a page of plastic over the back cover, with an even border all round. Mark through the punched holes along the spine with a nail. Hammer holes through the cover at marked points with a nail, making sure to place a piece of wood under the plastic.

five To create a frame for your 3D object, cut the polyboard on a cutting mat using a craft knife and metal ruler.

six Stick the frame onto a page of card stock. Leave to dry. Line the recess with fabric or paper that will complement the object you are framing.

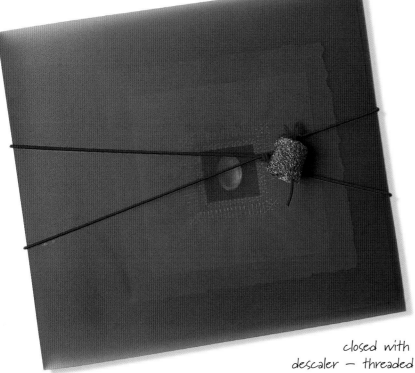

LEFT Frosted plastic book covers have become very fashionable. This book is kept closed with an inventive fastener — a kettle descaler — threaded onto purple elastic.

seven Lay two pieces of paper on top of each other – the bottom one cut slightly wider – to create a pretty border that conceals the frame by at least ½ in (1½ cm) on the inside and ¾ in (2 cm) on the outside. Embellish the top border with embossing liquid. Use epoxy glue to stick your 3D object into the recess.

nine Thread elastic through the holes on the plastic back cover and through each page. Add the polyboard space next to the page with the 3D object. Tie the ends into a bow.

ten Make a long loop of elastic big enough to wrap around your album. Tie a knot in the loose ends 4 in (10 cm) from the end. Thread the loose ends through the kettle descaler to make the fastener, conceal the knot inside. Trim off excess length.

eight To create enough space for your 3D object, cut a wedge of polyboard the same thickness as the margin, but shorter and narrower. Paste pretty paper over it and leave to dry. Punch holes in it with a leather punch to line up with the holes on the pages.

RIGHT Whatever your special find is – be it a shell, seed pod, or fragile leaf – keep it safe in this cleverly designed album.

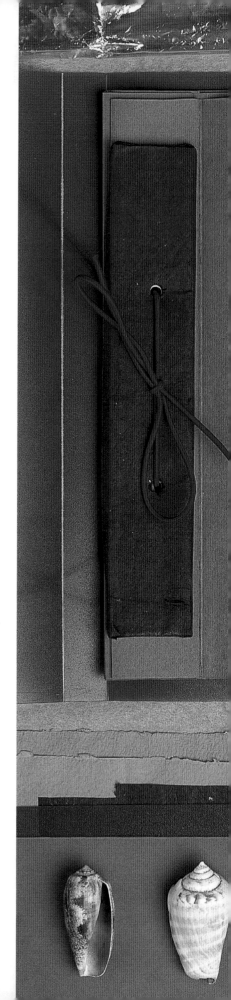

Making collector's pockets

one Glue colored strips of paper onto the page.

two Glue down smaller translucent strips and punch four holes through the page with a hole punch.

three Place the beads onto a plastic sheet, then fold up the sheet to make a small package.

four Place the package on the translucent paper. Thread silver ribbon from the back through the side hole, over the top of the package to the other side hole. Twist at the back and thread two ends up through the end holes. Tie securely.

ABOVE It's possible to make some really stunning envelopes with simple paper and ribbon — all you need is to know how.

Copper Envelope

LEFT The gleam of copper paper and copper embossing fluid make this purple page look sumptuous. But it's not only beautiful to look at — you can store any precious items in the envelope you have made.

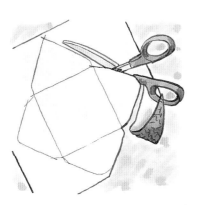

one Cut envelope from copper paper 12 x 12 in (30 x 30 cm), as shown above.

two Stick three edges down, making sure you use glue only where the three flaps overlap.

three Stick the envelope onto the page with craft glue and emboss the page with swirls of copper embossing liquid.

More collector's pockets

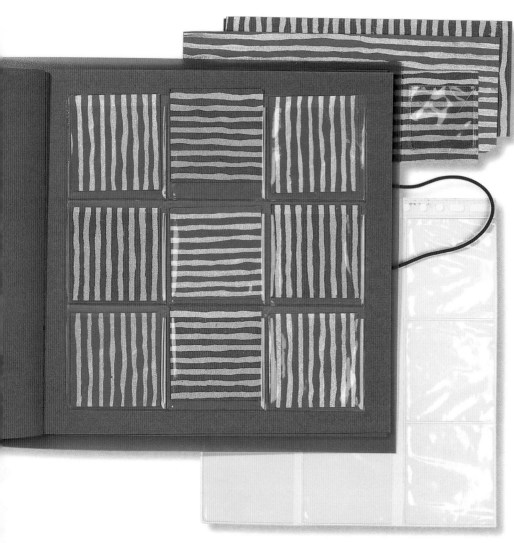

LEFT Create eye-catching background paper for your pockets, cleverly made from slide holders, and store your precious finds safely.

one Stick slide holder onto the page with plastic-compatible glue.

two Decorate colored paper with gold and silver marker pens or ink.

three Fill the pockets with decorated paper and add your mementoes.

Making a photo grid

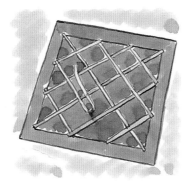

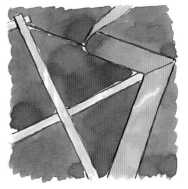

one Stick a square of fabric onto the page with glue.

two Criss-cross strips of silver thread or elastic diagonally across the material about 2 in (5 cm) apart.

three Secure with copper sticky tape around the edge of the material and insert your photos and postcards.

RIGHT This page looks like a noticeboard on a wall — perfect for storing vacation photos or postcards from friends. And it's easy to add in or take out more whenever you wish.

Carry-all Book

This book with its pages of pockets, envelopes, and elastic holders has been specially designed to contain loose or bulky items. The pages are easily threaded onto an elastic binding which is tied to allow you to remove or add pages.

Materials and equipment

- POLYBOARD WITH FOAM CORE 24¹/2x9¹/2 IN (62x24 CM)
- SHEET OF COVER PAPER
- CRAFT GLUE (P.V.A.)
- BOOKCLOTH TAPE
- LINING PAPER
- ROUND ELASTIC
- SHEETS OF HANDMADE PAPER 8x11 IN (20x28 CM)
- THREAD AND NEEDLE
- BIAS TAPE
- PLASTIC STONE-EFFECT BEAD
- METAL RULER
- CRAFT KNIFE
- AWL AND BONE FOLDER
- HAMMER AND NAIL

CREATE THE BOOK

one To make the book's spine, score two parallel lines 1¼ in (3 cm) apart down the center of the polyboard, cutting through the first layer of card and foam. Fold into book shape.

two Cut cover paper to size and paste into position. Smooth out creases with the bone folder. Leave under a telephone directory or heavy book to dry. Paste on cover decoration.

three Fold the cover into position. Stick the book cloth tape along the spine, working it into the cut channels and around the side. Cut slits into the tape at the corners so that you can fold in over the top and bottom edges. Line the inside spine with the same tape.

four Cut the lining paper to size, avoiding the spine. Paste into position and leave to dry. Tape an even border of book cloth all around and over the edges of the front and back covers.

BELOW Interesting handmade paper has been cut and torn, and mounted onto the cover of this album. The bamboo leaves embedded into the paper suggest an oriental feel.

seven Oversew along the spine with diagonal stitches. When one length is completed, work back the other way to form cross stitches.

eight Thread a length of bias tape through this stitching.

five Hammer three sets of holes with a nail into the corners of three of the squares on the paper to form crosses. Thread elastic through the holes from the back forming crosses at the front.

six Group six sheets of paper together and, with the awl, pierce holes ⅜ in (1 cm) in from the spine edge, at 3½ in (9 cm) intervals. Repeat with the other pages.

nine Position the pages in place between the covers, then wrap the bias tape around the outside of the book and tie in a bow along the spine.

RIGHT This page was bought from a good paper supplier with squares of other papers already incorporated into it. You could create a similar look by cutting out squares of paper and pasting them onto a background sheet of paper.

ten Thread some round elastic through the plastic bead and secure with a knot. Thread the loop under the spine tape and around the book cover, allowing enough elastic for the bead to hook into the loop tightly to close the book securely.

RAFFIA POCKETS AND GRID

ABOVE To create an interesting page for inclusions, cut pocket files to size. Line each pocket with handmade paper and stitch the pockets in place using raffia. Continue the stitches around the back to create a raffia grid. Tie the ends of the raffia to secure them.

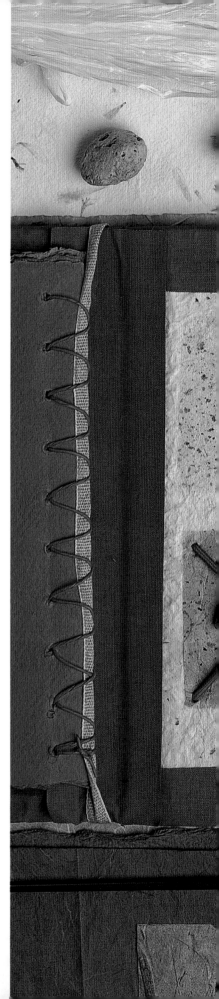

Chapter 3

MAKING BOOKS

Once you've learned to embellish and personalize covers and inside pages, its only a small step to making your own albums and journals from scratch. The following ten projects outline — with clear, illustrated step-by-step instructions — the different methods you can use to bind together pages and albums, journals, folders or notebooks. When you have mastered the techniques, you can create keepsakes and gift books to your own design.

Spiral-bound Dream Book

Wired-up plastic tubing and translucent plastic combine to make this unusual dream book. With its "glow-in-the-dark" star, it'll be easy to find at night to record your latest dream.

Materials and equipment

- 3 SHEETS OF TRANSLUCENT PLASTIC OR ACETATE 11X11 IN (28X28 CM)

- 8X8 IN (20X20 CM) BLUE/GREEN/MAUVE NOTEPAD

- 18 IN (45 CM) OF GALVANIZED GARDEN WIRE AND OF 1/4 IN (6 MM) WIDE PLASTIC TUBING

- CRAFT GLUE (P.V.A.)

- 2 LARGE BEADS

- LARGE FLUORESCENT STAR

- MATTE SILVER FOIL

- DOUBLE-SIDED CARPET TAPE

- SCISSORS

- RULER AND PENCIL

- MASKING TAPE

- 2 THIN STRIPS OF WOOD 8X1 IN (20X1 1/2 CM)

- 2 "G" CLAMPS

- DRILL WITH 1/4 IN (6MM) SPUR BIT

- THICK DOWEL ROD

CREATE THE BOOK

one Cut three plastic sheets with scissors as follows. Back cover: 8 x 8 in (20 x 20 cm). Divider: same size as first, but cut away a ¾ in (2 cm) border on three sides. Front cover: same size as back cover, but cut away a 1¼ in (3 cm) border on three sides.

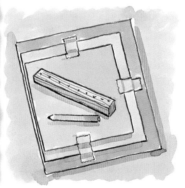

two Place the three sheets on top of each other, lining them up at the left edge where the spiral tubing will be. Make sure the borders are even around the other three sides. Secure with masking tape. Mark points for drilling holes at ¾ in (2 cm) intervals. Mark the same points on the pad and on one of the battens.

three Tape the pad and plastic sheets, lining up all the markings. Clamp them between the battens with the marked points on top. Drill the holes.

four Insert the wire through the plastic tubing (available from hardware or aquarium stores). Drill a hole in the end of a dowel rod and mark ¾ in (2 cm) intervals. Insert wire into the hole and wrap the tubing around the stick to make a spiral coil to the required length.

five Split the notepad in half and insert the plastic divider. Add the front and back covers. Line up all the holes and insert the plastic tubing in the holes, carefully winding it on. Trim off excess tubing, leaving ¾ in (2 cm) of wire at each end. Bend these into right angles and glue a bead onto each end.

ABOVE Keep a record of your unconscious thoughts in this special dream book with its "glow-in-the-dark" star

six Decorate the front of the pad with the glowing star. Back the silver foil with double-sided carpet tape and cut into little squares. Stick around the inside of the back plastic cover so that they show through as a border.

Suede Notepad

Made from soft supple suede and special Khadi paper in shades of brown and russet, this stylish book just begs to be used. Continue the organic theme by recording nature notes in it or displaying pressed flowers or leaves. Use new suede or old — try recycling suede from an old jacket or skirt.

Materials and equipment

- 34x22 IN (87x56 CM) PIECE OF SUEDE
- KHADI PAPER, ABOUT 21 SHEETS 10 1/2x8 IN (27x20 CM)
- BUTTON THREAD
- BEESWAX
- SUEDE THONGING
- DUFFLE COAT TOGGLE
- PENCIL
- RULER
- AWL
- LEATHER OR DARNING NEEDLE
- SCISSORS

CREATE THE BOOK

one Fold the suede in half widthways (leather side facing up), and lightly mark a pencil line down the center.

two From this line make seven lines either side, each 1/4 in (6 mm) apart.

three Mark out points along each line, midway and 1 1/4 in (3 cm) from the top and bottom. Make holes using the awl. This will form the spine.

four Fold each sheet of Khadi paper in half, leaving its natural deckle edging intact. Nestle three folded sheets inside each other. Make seven of these "signatures."

ABOVE Khadi paper is a roughly textured handmade paper with natural deckle edging, available from good arts and crafts stores. Used here, it enhances the notepad's organic look and feel.

five Mark points along the paper to match the spine holes (see step three). Thread the needle and draw a long piece of button thread through the beeswax. Take one paper signature and align it with the seven pencil lines on the inside of the suede cover. Stitch from inside the pages through the suede. At the top hole run the thread along the outside of cover.

six Insert the needle back through the cover at the bottom hole, across the inside pages and out through the center hole. Take the needle around the previous stitch and back through the center hole.

seven Tie the ends of thread together with a square knot (left over right, and right over left) and trim the ends. Repeat with the remaining six signatures.

RIGHT Recycled suede has been used to make the cover of this notepad, which is kept secure by a wooden toggle attached to a suede thong. An unusual piece of branch has been tucked into the ties for decoration.

eight Measure and cut a length of thonging to wrap around the book two and a half times.

nine Double it and thread the ends, from the back, under the spine stitches either side of the center. Leave the loop projecting from the back cover to act as the buttonhole.

ten Tie the toggle into place at the edge of the front cover. Button up the book to get the correct length before snipping off excess.

Scallop Shell Book

Flat scallop shells form a witty little book to write down poems, impressions, or special thoughts. The pages have been roughly torn out of mottled paper to add to the organic nature of the book and the elastic binding allows it to open flat. To finish, the shells were burnished with metallic wax, adding that special touch.

Materials and equipment

- 2 SAME-SIZE FLAT SCALLOP SHELLS (AVAILABLE FROM CRAFT SUPPLIERS OR SEAFOOD STORES)

- MOTTLED OR SPECKLED PAPER IN SEASHORE HUES

- ROUND ELASTIC OR RIBBON

- GOLD/ SILVER METALLIC WAX AND SOFT CLOTH

- PENCIL

- PUTTY (BLU-TAK)

- CLAMP

- DRILL AND FINE BIT

- HOLE PUNCH

- SCISSORS

CREATE THE BOOK

one Use a pencil to mark two evenly placed slots on the flat end of each scallop. Secure the scallops with putty. Clamp and drill the holes in the marked points.

two Draw round one of the shells onto the mottled paper and mark out the holes.

three Tear out the shell shapes so that you have rough edges. You will need about 50 shell-shaped sheets for the book.

four Make holes with a hole punch using a size to suit your binding elastic or ribbon – possibly ⅛ in (3 mm) punch.

five Thread the elastic or ribbon from the bottom shell through all the pages and the top cover shell.

ABOVE Roughly torn pages are sandwiched between two flat scallop shells to make a clever and organic little book.

six Cross the elastic or ribbon over the spine of the book, then insert it through the second set of holes.

seven Tie the two remaining ends into a knot around the diagonal elastic, forming a cross. Make sure this is secure before trimming off the ends.

eight Using a soft cloth, buff the scallop shells with gold or silver metallic wax.

RIGHT Each scallop shell is unique with its own special markings — that's what makes them a perfect choice for a one-of-a-kind natural notebook.

VARIATION

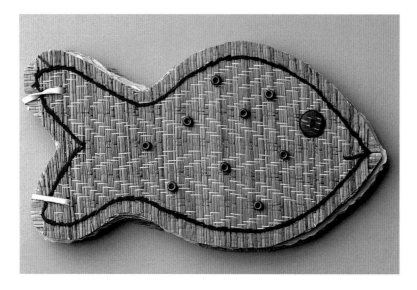

ABOVE Use an old straw beach mat and speckled paper to make an organic fish-shaped notebook to jot down your beach impressions.

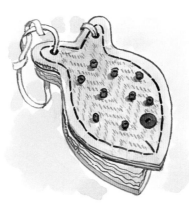

one Using a fish template, cut eight identical fish shapes from the beach mat. Layer four of the fish on top of each other and sew around the fish shape with strong wool in back stitch ⅜ in (1 cm) from the edge. Repeat for the back cover. Cut fish-shaped paper.

two Make two small holes in the tails of each fish with the point of a sharp knife. Sew on a button for the eye of the fish and sew beads on at random. Insert pages between the covers. Thread elastic through the covers and pages and tie securely.

Lovers' Album

Remnants of luscious lavender, purple, and peach materials have been brought together to form this richly textured album. The simple binding uses post fittings — available from specialist suppliers — which allow pages to be added or removed.

Materials and equipment

- 20x15 IN (50x38 CM) SHEET OF STIFF CARDBOARD

- OPEN WEAVE GAUZE BANDAGE

- CRAFT GLUE (P.V.A.)

- 30x12 IN (80x30 CM) SILK FOR COVER

- 30x12 IN (80x30 CM) LINING FABRIC

- 5 IN (13 CM) SQUARE OF VELVET

- 15x12 IN (38x30 CM) LIGHT-WEIGHT IRON-ON INTERFACING

- 6x7 IN (15x18 CM) PATCH OF FABRIC

- STRIP OF WEBBING (BONDAWEB)

MATERIALS LIST CONTINUES ON FOLLOWING PAGE

CREATE THE BOOK

one Cut two squares from the cardboard sized 10 x 10 in (25 x 25 cm) and two strips 10 x 1½ in (25 x 4 cm). Pair up each strip with a square. Join them together by gluing a length of open weave bandage across them using craft glue, leaving a ¼ in (6 mm) gap in between.

two Cut out two rectangles of fabric for the outside covers sized 15 x 12 in (38 x 30 cm) and two for the inside cover 9¾ x 14¾ in (24½ x 42½ cm). Cut the square of velvet into a heart shape. Back each piece with iron-on interfacing and iron as directed.

three Take the patch of fabric and fray the edges by about ½ in (1 cm). Using the webbing, iron it onto the middle of the cover fabric. Stitch round it using embroidery thread.

LEFT Once the screws have been undone from this post-bound album, you can add or take away pages of your choice.

seven Carefully turn the cover over. Stick double-sided carpet tape around the edge of the inside cover. Trim off corners and cut away the joint between the cover and the spine. Fold in edging, attaching it to the tape, making sure the cover is taut and even. Repeat on the other cover.

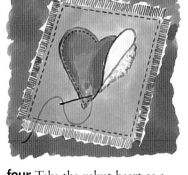

five Using a fine beading needle and a simple stitch, sew the sequins to the heart. Secure them with a small bead. Space them evenly around the patch.

four Take the velvet heart as a guide and cut out a heart shape from the smaller square of batting. Using running stitch, sew the heart to the cover, sandwiching the batting.

six Pad the cover using the larger square of batting. Spread a thin layer of craft glue over the cover interfacing and lay the batting in position. The heart should be central to the wadding. Smooth any creases along the strip end.

eight Once the covers are dry you can line them with fabric. Spread craft glue over the lining fabrics and position the covers carefully. Make sure you smooth out any creases with a bone folder. While the books are drying, place a medium-weight book over them to keep them flat.

Materials and equipment continued

- EMBROIDERY THREAD

- 2 X SQUARES OF BATTING ¼ IN (6 MM) THICK: 9½ IN (24 CM) SQUARE & 5 IN (13 CM) SQUARE

- STAR SEQUIN

- SMALL GLASS BEADS

- DOUBLE-SIDED CARPET TAPE

- CARD STOCK

- 5 X A1 SHEETS OF CARD STOCK FOR PAGES

- 2 X ENDPAPERS 10X12 IN (40X30 CM)

- SCISSORS

- PENCIL

- RULER

- SEWING NEEDLE

- FINE BEADING NEEDLE

- BONE FOLDER

- LEATHER PUNCH

- PHOTOGRAPHIC METAL MOUNTING POSTS WITH SCREW HEADS

RIGHT A red velvet heart is appliquéd on to the front of this padded silk album cover, designed to hold your innermost feelings and precious photographs.

nine Using a leather punch, create holes evenly spaced along the cover strip 6 in (15 cm) apart. Cut out about 20 sheets of card stock 11 x 9½ in (28 x 24 cm). Score a margin 1½ in (4 cm) in each and turn them in. Punch holes ¾ in (2 cm) in from the edge 6 in (15 cm) apart to match the cover.

ten Cut two 9½ in (24 cm) square endpapers (reinforce the holes if necessary). Insert the metal mounting posts through the holes on the inside of the base cover. Then fold over the margin strip. Thread the endpaper on first followed by the pages, and finally the front endpaper. Put on the cover, fit the screw heads to secure it, and fold the back cover.

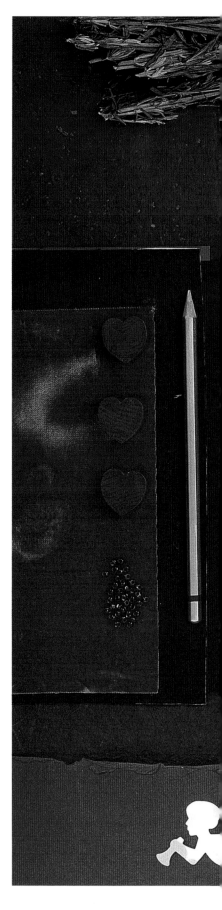

Japanese Album

Pressed flowers make lovely decorations, especially if they've been picked from your own garden or on a walk. This album has been bound in the Japanese style with tortoiseshell stitching, using button thread.

Materials and equipment

- FINE HANDMADE PAPERS
- CRAFT GLUE (P.V.A.)
- PRESSED FLOWERS
- 26 IN (66 CM) SQUARE OF THICK CARDBOARD
- OPEN WEAVE GAUZE BANDAGE
- 4 SHEETS OF COVER PAPER 18x16 IN (46x40 CM)
- 20 SHEETS OF COLORED ART CARD STOCK 16x12 IN (40x30 CM)
- GLUE STICK
- BUTTON THREAD
- BEESWAX
- CRAFT KNIFE
- METAL RULER
- SCISSORS
- BONE FOLDER
- AWL
- NEEDLE

CREATE THE BOOK

one Tear two squares of fine handmade paper and paste them together with craft glue to make the base for your flower plaque. Leave to dry. Apply your pressed flowers to the plaque with slightly diluted craft glue.

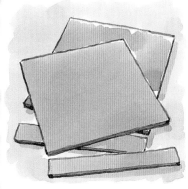

two Using a strong craft knife and metal ruler, cut two 12 in (30 cm) squares of board and two 12 x 2 in (30 x 5 cm) rectangles.

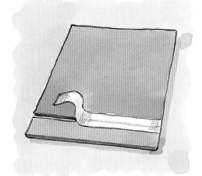

three Cut two strips of gauze 12¼ in (31 cm) long. Arrange each square of card and oblong next to each other with a ¼ in (5 mm) gap between. Join these cards by pasting the gauze evenly down the gap.

four Paste one sheet of cover paper onto the front, leaving a 2½ in (6½ cm) overlap on the spine side. Snip the outer corners, turn and paste in the edges. Repeat on the other cover. Leave to dry under a telephone directory or two.

ABOVE Pressed dried flowers are incorporated into the handmade paper that lines the book's inside covers. Sheets of acid-free tissue paper can be interspersed between the pages to protect photographs.

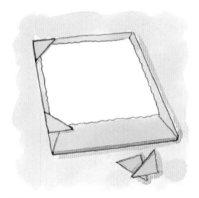

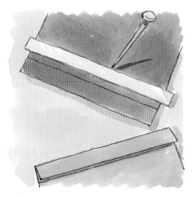

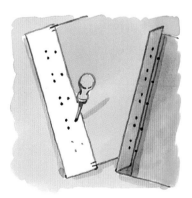

five Glue cover paper in place for the inside covers and paste the corners over for decoration. Repeat on second cover. Leave to dry, weighted as before.

six Take the sheets of colored card stock and, using the short side, score two margins 2 in (5 cm) apart. Turn the first of these over and crease into place using a bone folder. Tear out two sheets for endpapers from handmade paper, tearing along the ruler to get a rough edge.

seven Mark holes along the second scored margin at 2 in (5 cm) intervals. Using an awl, make holes at the marked points. Allow an extra ¼ in (6 mm) on either side of the edges of the cover boards, as they are larger.

LEFT To prepare the flowers for the cover, pick them at their prime and press them between two sheets of blotting paper under heavy weights for at least a month. Protect the cover by keeping the album in a box, so that the flowers don't fade.

nine Using thick button thread pulled through beeswax, stitch as shown below. To finish, tie up the ends of thread inside the cover.

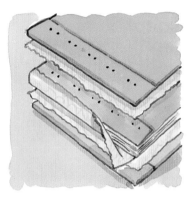

eight Put the pages and endpapers together. Cut a strip of endpaper 12 x 2½ in (30 x 6½ cm). Wrap around the spine and hold in place with a glue stick. Put the covers in position.

ten Paste the flower plaque on to the front cover. Decorate with watercolor paints or extra torn paper tucked under the stitching if you wish. Place a sheet of paper over the plaque and leave it under a book to dry.

JAPANESE BINDING

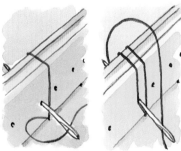

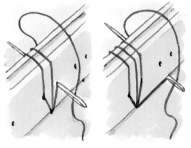

one/two From the back, push needle through the second hole on the crease. Bring thread over the spine edge to the back, and push needle through the main hole. Push needle through the left hole and back over the spine.

three/four Repeat the stitch for the hole to the right of the first stitch. Bring thread back through the main hole and move it across to the next main hole. Repeat the whole process until you have filled all the holes.

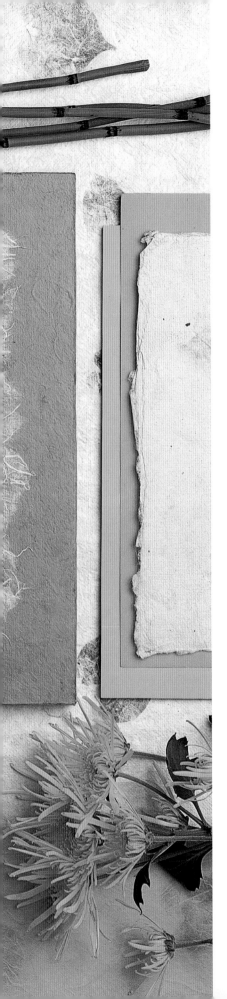

Felt Notebook

Here a loose felt cover, simply stitched, brings a special look to an inexpensive jotter that's reminiscent of the 1940s and 1950s. The end-papers and motif, were chosen to complement the design and color scheme.

Materials and equipment

- 6x4 IN (15x10 CM) NOTEBOOK

- SHEET OF ENDPAPER 24x16 IN (60x40 CM)

- CRAFT GLUE (P.V.A.)

- 12 IN (30 CM) SQUARES IN BLACK, DARK GREEN, AND LIGHT GREEN FELT

- 2 GREEN BUTTONS

- LIGHT GREEN AND BLACK COTTON THREAD

- THICK EMBROIDERY THREAD IN BLACK AND YELLOW

- METAL RULER

- SCISSORS

- BONE FOLDER

- PINKING SHEARS

- NEEDLE

- CRAFT KNIFE

CREATE THE LOOK

one Cut two sheets sized 11½ x 7½ in (29 x 19 cm) from the endpaper. Paste one sheet over the inside back cover, smoothing in place with the bone folder. Make sure that you work into the groove at the spine. Leave to dry then repeat with inside front cover.

two Cut a piece 10½ x 6¾ in (27 x 17 cm) from the black felt. Using pinking shears, cut a piece 10¼ x 6¾ in (26 x 17 cm) from the dark green felt. Cut a piece 9¾ x 6¼ in (25½ x 16 cm) from the light green felt.

three Make a leaf design template by folding a sheet of paper in half. Then draw a leaf shape using the fold as the center vein and cut out a symmetrical shape.

four Wrap the light green felt around the notebook. Mark the motif position on the front and back covers. Draw around the leaf template on the felt and cut out two shapes.

RIGHT Elephants are always popular. Cut two pieces of felt into an elephant shape and stitch them together. Cut a slit into the back of the elephant and stuff with cotton or scrap felt. Sew up the slit and add details with beads, ribbons, and embroidery thread. Sew onto the front cover.

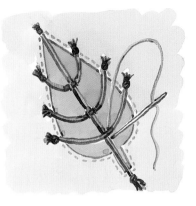

five Place the light green felt over the dark green, making an even zigzag border. Stitch the felts together around the leaf shapes with light green cotton. Make leaf veins from thick black embroidery thread, each one longer than the leaf and tie a knot in each end. Secure in place with black and green cotton.

six Place the green leaves on the black felt (this will line the inside front cover). Paste the leaves in position using craft glue. Make veins and stitch them on as before, using light yellow thread.

seven Using a metal ruler and craft knife, cut two parallel lines 6 x 1½ in (15 x 4 cm) apart down the center of the black felt. Apply a little craft glue to the back of the strip and place it over the cover's spine, between the leaf shapes. Leave to dry.

VARIATION

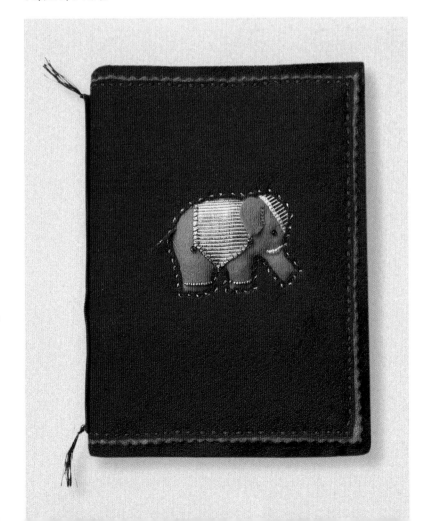

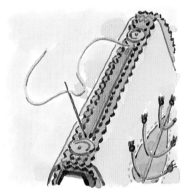

eight Using pinking shears, cut a strip of dark green felt 6¼ x 1 in (16 x 2½ cm) wide and one in black 6 x ½ in (15 x 1½ cm). Lay these over the black felt spine. Stitch a green button at the top with light green embroidery thread. Take one straight stitch along the spine, then stitch the other button at the bottom. Take another long stitch back to the top. Tie the thread off on the underside.

RIGHT AND BELOW Beneath this slip-on cover is an ordinary notebook bought from a stationery supplier. The jacket has been made with layers of felt and features a simple leaf shape sewn on with running stitch. Complementary endpapers have been added to the inside of the book, as seen below.

nine To make the inside cover, place the black felt in position. Sew a running stitch all around the edge of the cover. Make sure that you allow enough room for your notebook covers to slide in.

ten Fold the covers of the notebook right back and slip them into the felt cover.

Accordion Book

Accordion books are widely used in the Far East and this book has an exotic Eastern feel with the black feather contrasting against the deep gold cover and bamboo leaves embedded in the pages. Use it to write beautiful poetry or prose with calligraphy.

Materials and equipment

- DENSE CARDBOARD OR HARDBOARD
- GOLD COVER PAPER
- CRAFT GLUE (P.V.A.)
- BLACK FEATHER
- 2 1/4 YARDS (2 M) BLACK BIAS TAPE
- 36X9 IN (100X23 CM) BAMBOO EMBELLISHED HANDMADE PAPER
- 1 IN (2 1/2 CM) WIDE ADHESIVE BOOK-CLOTH TAPE
- CREAM BINDING TAPE
- METAL RULER
- CRAFT KNIFE
- PENCIL
- BONE FOLDER

CREATE THE BOOK

one Cut two rectangles 10 x 4¾ in (25 x 12 cm) from the cardboard for the book covers. Cut two sheets of gold cover paper, slightly smaller.

two Using craft glue, stick the cover paper to the outside of the cardboard covers. Smooth them down using the bone folder.

VARIATION

three Stick the feather to the front cover with craft glue. Place a telephone directory or heavy book on top and leave until dry.

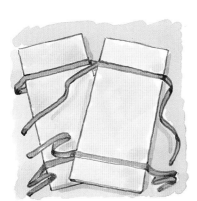

four Cut four lengths of black bias tape about 20 in (50 cm) long. Glue these to the inside covers to run across the width in parallel pairs 2½ in (6½ cm) from the top and bottom.

five Cut a long strip of hand-made paper 24 x 9 in (60 x 23 cm). Increase the length by 4 in (10 cm) per page for more pages. Mark out intervals 4 in (10 cm) along the length on both sides.

six Score and fold on alternate sides so that the paper will fold easily, accordion style.

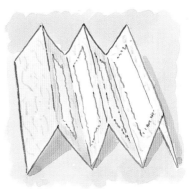

seven Depending on your usage and paper, you may wish to line these pages by pasting smaller pieces of paper on top. Here, we added handmade paper with roughly torn edges to one side of the book.

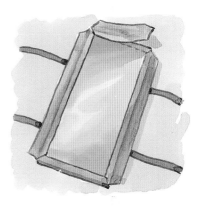

eight Cut two lengths of adhesive book-cloth tape 10 in (25 cm) long and two lengths 4¾ in (12 cm) for each cover. Faintly mark a ¼ in (6 cm) edging around the outside covers and stick the tape along these borders. Cut corners diagonally for a neat finish.

LEFT Recycle common household items to create a strikingly different cover for an accordian book. Cut a sheet of 1 in (2½ cm) tile spacers — available from a hardware store — to form a square with 16 recesses. Stick the square onto your front cover with strong glue. Paint the tile spacers with craft glue and stick torn strips of creased white tissue paper over the square, pushing the tissue into the corners with a paint brush. Repeat until you have three layers. Finally, use strong glue to fix decorations of your choice into the 16 recesses. Beaded flowers, as shown here, are a pretty option.

ABOVE
AND RIGHT
It makes a refreshing change
when a book opens in an unusual way. This
accordion book with its concertina folds is tied
together at the side with black binding tape and a
stylish feather decorates the front cover.

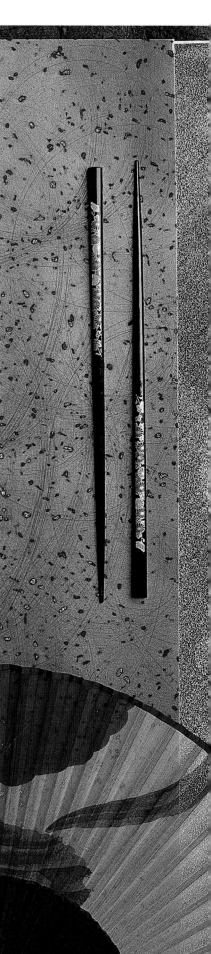

nine Turn each cover over and cut slits – matching the black tapes – into the sticky tape, using a scalpel. Slot the tapes through the slits. Continue to stick tape along the edge and inside.

ten Attach the ends of the accordion paper to the inside of both covers with craft glue. Glue a strip of binding tape along the edges to cover the joints. Cut corners diagonally for a neat finish. Leave both covers under a heavy book to dry.

Copper Jotter

In this unusual and exotic book, turquoise foil glitters through punched copper covers. You could even use a copper ink pen to write your special thoughts.

Materials and equipment

- SOFT TEMPERED COPPER SHIM 8x6 IN (20x15 CM)
- COPPER AND TURQUOISE COLORED FOIL
- CRAFT GLUE (P.V.A.)
- TURQUOISE TISSUE PAPER
- CARDBOARD 8¹/2x6¹/4 IN (22x16 CM)
- EPOXY ADHESIVE
- ³/4 IN (2 CM) AND 2 IN (5 CM) WIDE BOOK CLOTH TAPE
- 71¹/4 IN (180 CM) OF ¹/4 IN (6 MM) DOWEL ROD
- COPPER PAINT, PAINTBRUSH, AND EMBOSSING LIQUID
- 15 SHEETS OF BLACK CARD STOCK 8¹/2x5 IN (22x 13 CM)
- 5 BEADS (2 LARGE)
- TIN SNIPS
- KNITTING NEEDLE
- HAMMER AND AWL
- CRAFT KNIFE AND METAL RULER

CREATE THE BOOK

one Using tin snips, cut the copper into two rectangles 6 x 4 in (15 x 10 cm). Place on a protected, yielding surface and punch random holes using an awl.

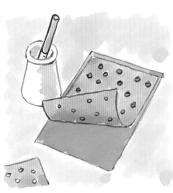

two Glue foil to the back of both copper covers and leave to dry.

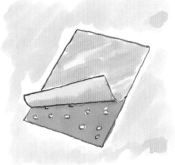

three To make the endpapers, punch holes in the turqoise tissue paper using a knitting needle. Paste copper colored foil onto the back of the tissue paper and leave to dry under a book.

four Cut two rectangles of cardboard slightly larger than the covers, using the craft knife and ruler. Glue each cover to each board using epoxy adhesive. Leave to dry under a directory or book. When dry, paste endpapers onto the inside cover and dry as before.

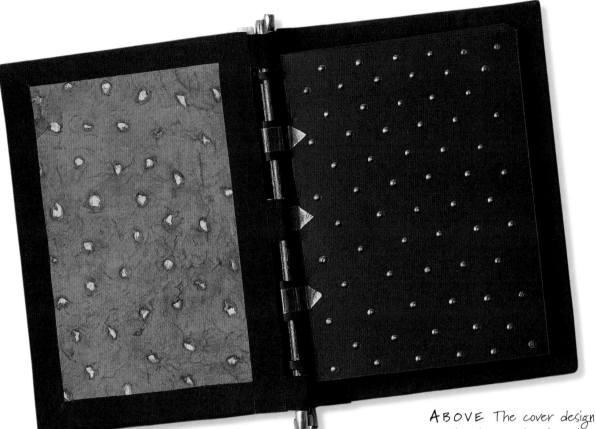

ABOVE The cover design has been echoed on the endpapers, where holes have been pierced in the turqoise tissue paper so that the copper-colored foil peeks through. You can continue the copper theme by embellishing your inside pages with copper embossing fluid.

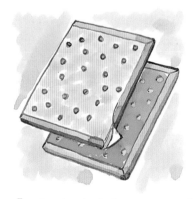

five Lay book cloth tape over and around the top, bottom, and one long side of each cover, giving a ³⁄₈ in (1 cm) border.

six For the fourth side, cut two lengths of 2 in (5 cm) wide book cloth tape. Remove ³⁄₈ in (1 cm) of the backing and stick it to the outside of each cover.

seven Cut slots in the tape as shown in the diagram, leaving tabs.

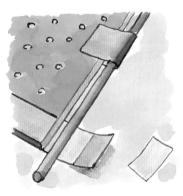

eight Cut five copper-painted dowel rods 8 in (20 cm) long. Loop the end tabs on each cover over the dowel. Remove ³/₈ in (1 cm) of the tape backing from the free end and stick the tab to the inside cover. Make alternate loops. One cover will have three loops, the other four. Stick ¾ in (2 cm) wide book cloth tape over the end tabs on the inside covers.

nine Score a vertical line down the center of each sheet of black card stock and fold. Make five groups of three sheets. Along the folds cut ½ in (1½ cm) slots with a metal ruler and craft knife, to make the spine tabs. Leaving the ⅛ in (3 mm) tabs at either end, cut away four of the intervals to create three ½ in (1½ cm) tabs.

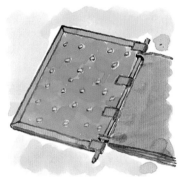

ten Paint five 6¼ in (16 cm) lengths of dowel rod with copper paint and leave to dry. Take the cover with three tabs, thread the rod through the cover and first signature. Fold the first tab, middle, and last tab away. Thread the rod through the cover tab, two tabs of second signature, the middle tab of the cover. Thread the second rod through the tabs that were folded back. Alternate the tabs from the second signature with the tabs from the first signature, so the tabs interlock like a hinge.

eleven Glue a small bead on the end of the middle dowel rods to stop them slipping. The first and last dowels feature larger beads. Stick copper foil to the spine tabs with epoxy adhesive. Decorate the inside pages with copper embossing liquid as desired.

RIGHT The overall effect of this copper book is faintly medieval. You can buy soft tempered copper shim from good hardware stores and craft suppliers — an alternative would be to use pewter or aluminum shim.

Handmade Paper Book

It's rare to find a book made up of many different types of paper, so why not make your own. This one is created from handmade paper (see recipes on pages 52–57) including watercolor and pastel papers. It is bound with a ribbon, so you can add or remove pages as required. Use the page offcuts to create a woven cover.

Materials and equipment

- 10 OR MORE SHEETS OF HANDMADE PAPERS
- DOUBLE-SIDED TAPE
- 2 SQUARE FOAM BOARDS 14 IN (35¹/2 CM)
- OPEN WEAVE GAUZE BANDAGE
- CRAFT GLUE (P.V.A.)
- GOLD PAPER
- RIBBON
- MASKING TAPE
- CRAFT KNIFE AND SCISSORS
- METAL RULER
- LEATHER PUNCH OR AWL
- HOLE PUNCH

CREATE THE BOOK

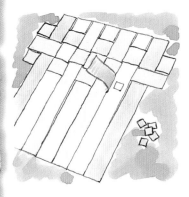

one Cut three sheets of different papers into fourteen strips 18 x 2 in (46 x 5 cm) long. Weave these together, holding them in place with tabs of double-sided tape. Allow a 2 in (5 cm) overlap all around the edge.

two Partially cut a 2 in (5 cm) margin through both foam boards. This will be the basis of the spine.

three Cut two 14 in (35½ cm) strips from the linen gauze. Paste each strip over the reverse side of the cut margin (outside cover) on both boards.

four Paste craft glue to the outside cover of the front board. Position the woven paper carefully on it before smoothing it into position. Choose an interesting piece of paper 18 in (45 cm) square for the back cover and paste in position. Place each cover under a telephone directory or heavy book to dry.

six Back gold paper with double-sided tape, snip into ¾ in (2 cm) squares. Apply to the center of each woven square for decoration.

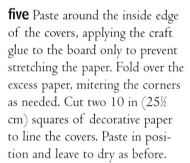

five Paste around the inside edge of the covers, applying the craft glue to the board only to prevent stretching the paper. Fold over the excess paper, mitering the corners as needed. Cut two 10 in (25½ cm) squares of decorative paper to line the covers. Paste in position and leave to dry as before.

BELOW The first page of the book echoes the unusual cover with strips of handmade paper interwoven to make a fine-textured grid, which is then pasted onto background paper.

seven Use a leather punch or awl to make two holes in the spine edge of each cover about 3 in (7½ cm) from the top and bottom and 1 in (2½ cm) from the edge.

eight Cut or tear about 16 pages of various papers about 12 x 11 in (30½ x 28 cm). Reinforce the spine edge of flimsy papers with a strip of masking tape. Punch corresponding holes in each sheet along one of the shorter edges. Thread a ribbon from the back cover, through the pages and front cover. Tie it into a bow and trim off any excess.

LEFT AND ABOVE The woven cover has been made from the offcuts of the inside pages and small gold squares were attached with double-sided tape. Inside (above), a flower arrangement made from pressed dried flowers and leaves is incorporated into the paper. The technique, called embossing, is explained on page 59.

Floral Fabric Scrapbook

This book is the perfect place to keep your sewing odds and ends. The pages are grouped into sections with floral fabric dividers, making it easy for you to find what you need. Add trimmings with tape, and stitch on buttons or beads.

Materials and equipment

- PIECE OF FIRM CARDBOARD 26X11 IN (66X28 CM)
- CRAFT GLUE (P.V.A.)
- OPEN WEAVE GAUZE
- VARIOUS COTTON FABRICS
- LINING FABRIC
- IRON—ON INTERFACING AND IRON
- 3 SHEETS THIN CARDBOARD 12X81/4 IN (30X21CM)
- 20 SHEETS CARD STOCK 12X81/4 IN (30X21 CM) IN VARIOUS COLORS
- BOOK CLOTH TAPE 2 IN (5 CM) WIDTH
- THICK ROUND ELASTIC
- CRAFT KNIFE AND METAL RULER
- SCISSORS
- BONE FOLDER
- AWL AND PAPER PUNCH

CREATE THE BOOK

one Cut two pieces of cardboard, each 13 x 8¼ in (33 x 21 cm) and two strips sized 13 x ¾ in (33 x 2 cm) using a metal ruler and craft knife.

two Pair each strip with the larger board, leaving a ¾ in (2 mm) gap between them. Glue each pair together using craft glue and gauze. These "bandaged" gaps will form the hinges of your book.

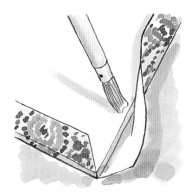

three Cut out two pieces of cotton fabric for the covers 16 x 13 in (40½ x 33 cm) and two pieces of lining fabric 10¼ x 7 in (26 x 18cm). Line each piece with lightweight iron-on interfacing. Remember to cover the interfacing with a cloth when ironing.

four Apply glue to the outside of the cardboard and place it onto the wrong side of the cover fabric. Turn over and smooth out any air bubbles with a bone folder. Snip the corners to miter them neatly and paste the edge over onto the inside. Repeat with the second cover. Leave to dry under heavy books or telephone directories.

five Once dry, paste the lining to the inside of each cover. Smooth out any bubbles and leave to dry as before.

six To make the dividers, cover three sheets of thin cardboard on each side with floral fabric (see step four). Using the templates shown here, cut out dividing tabs. Create a flexible edge by taping the book cloth around the spine edge of each divider, so that it overlaps the edge of the card by 1 in (2½ cm).

LEFT Use this book as a scrapbook for snippets of favorite material or bits and pieces that evoke a special memory and will inspire your sewing projects.

BELOW AND RIGHT The elasticated spiral binding allows the book to "bulk out" when fabric and buttons or bows are added. You could add an extra fastener — such as a ribbon — to keep the book shut if it's bursting at the seams.

seven Mark the spine holes on the covers, dividers, and sheets of card stock. These should be ¼ in (6 mm) from the edge and ¾ in (2 cm) apart. Use the awl for the covers and dividers, and a paper punch for the card.

eight Compile the pages, inserting the dividers as needed. Bind the spine together by threading thick round elastic spirally through the holes. Tie a knot in each end to secure.

Suppliers

Check your local telephone directory or the company web site for the location nearest you.

NORTH AMERICA

CraftCo Industries, Inc.
410 Wentworth Street North
Hamilton, Ontario
Canada L8L 5W3
Web site:
http://www.craftco.com

Hobby Lobby
7707 SW 44th Street
Oklahoma City, OK 73179
Tel: (405) 745-1100
Web site:
http://www.hobbylobby.com

Michael's Arts & Crafts
8000 Bent Branch Drive
Irving, TX 75063
Tel: (214) 409-1300
Web site:
http://www.michaels.com

Pearl Paint
308 Canal Street
New York, NY 10013
Tel: (212) 431-7931
Web site:
http://www.pearlpaint.com

Decorative Paper and Stationery Supplies:

Aiko's Art Materials Import
3347 N. Clark Street
Chicago, IL 60657
Tel: (312) 404-5600
Fax: (312) 404-5919

Dolphin Papers
1125 Brookside Avenue G-900
Indianapolis, IN 46202
Toll free: (800) 346-2770
Tel: (317) 634-0506
Fax: (317) 634-1370

Kate's Paperie
1282 Third Ave
New York, NY 10021
Tel: (212) 396-3670
Fax: (212) 941-9560
Web site:
http://www.katespaperie.com

The Paper Source
232 W. Chicago Avenue
Chicago, IL 60610
Tel: (312) 337-0798
Fax: (312) 337-0741

Papyrus
2500 N. Watney Way
Fairfield, CA 94533
Tel: (800) 333-6724
Web site:
http://www.papyrus-stores.com

Rugg Road Paper
105 Charles Street
Boston, MA 02114
Tel: (617) 742-0002

Beads and Findings:

Beadworks
290 Thayer Street
Providence, RI 02906
Tel: (401) 861-4540

UNITED KINGDOM

Daler-Rowney
P.O. Box 10, Bracknell
Berkshire R612 8ST
Tel: 01344 424 621
Fax: 01344 860 746
Web site:
http://www.daler-rowney.com

Specialist papers:

Faulkiner Fine Papers Ltd.
76 Southampton Row
London WC1B 4AR
Tel: 020 7831 1151
Fax: 020 7430 1248

Fabric, lace, ribbons, beads:

John Lewis plc
Oxford Street
London W1A 1EX
Tel: 020 7629 7711
Fax: 020 7514 5319
Web site:
http://www.johnlewis.co.uk

AUSTRALIA

Peninsula Plaza Arts Supplies
20 Bungan St, Mona Vale
NSW 2103
Tel: (02) 9979 6559

Fabric, lace, ribbons, beads:

Scarlet Ribbons Needlecraft
45 Kiwan Street
Floreat, Western Ausralia 6014
Tel: (08) 9383 9073
Fax: (08) 9383 9074
Web site:
http://lerner@ca.com.au

Glossary

Awl – pointed metal implement with wooden handles, useful for making preparatory holes through layers of paper, card stock, or cardboard.

Batten – a long flat strip of wood.

Batting – layers or sheets of raw cotton, wool, or synthetic fibrous material used for lining quilts or for stuffing or packaging.

Bias tape – a narrow strip of cloth cut on the bias, folded, and used for finishing or decorating clothing.

Bone folder – a tool made from a smooth, lozenge-shaped piece of bone. It is used to make folds in paper and card stock, or for smoothing out creases and air bubbles in pasted lining paper.

Bookcloth – paper-backed fabric used for book covers.

Bookcloth tape – tape backed with adhesive, used to cover a book spine or bind cover borders.

Couching – in papermaking, the process of transferring a freshly made sheet of paper from the mold surface onto a dampened felt.

Deckle edge scissors – scissors with blades for making a deckle-edged cut, such as a scalloped edge.

Dowel rod – a headless peg of wood, metal, or plastic for holding together components of a structure.

Embossing – the process of creating a raised or depressed design from a surface.

Embossing liquid – liquid used to add a three-dimensional quality to a page or cover.

Endpaper – a folded sheet, one leaf of which is pasted to the front or back of a hardcover book. The other leaf is pasted to the first or last page of the book.

Fabric photo – a photo that has been transferred onto fabric, usually cotton.

Felt – in papermaking, the woven woolen blanket onto which a newly formed sheet of paper is transferred or couched.

Iron-on interfacing – double-sided tape or fabric with adhesive, ironed on to strengthen and stiffen fabric.

Leather punch – a rotating punch, used for making holes in stiff or thick materials.

Mold – A rectangular wooden frame covered with a sieve-like laid or wove wire surface, used for sheet-forming in papermaking.

Photographic mounting spray – type of adhesive glue used to paste photographs into albums.

Pinking shears – shears with a saw-toothed inner edge on the blades for making a zigzag cut.

Polyboard (also *foam board* or *foam core*) – foam sandwiched between two pieces of cardboard, frequently used for the covers of books.

Post – a stack of newly formed paper sheets alternated with couching felts, ready for pressing.

Post bound album – an album containing punched pages held together by metal posts.

Pressing – in papermaking, the process of pressing paper to remove as much water as possible before drying, and to help bond the fibers into a strong sheet.

Raffia – the fiber from the leaves of a Madagascar palm tree, *Raphia ruffia*, used for cloths, hats, and baskets.

Shim – a thin often tapered piece of material (wood, metal, or stone) used to fill in space between things (as for support, levelling, adjustment of fit).

Vat – container for pulp in which sheets of paper are made.

Webbing – strong, narrow, closely woven fabric.

Index

Credits

Quarto and the author would like to thank and acknowledge
the following for their contributions to this book:

Sylvie McCracken for designing and making the variation projects
on pages 37, 46, 48, 94, 105, and 108.

Michael Wicks for his inspirational photography.

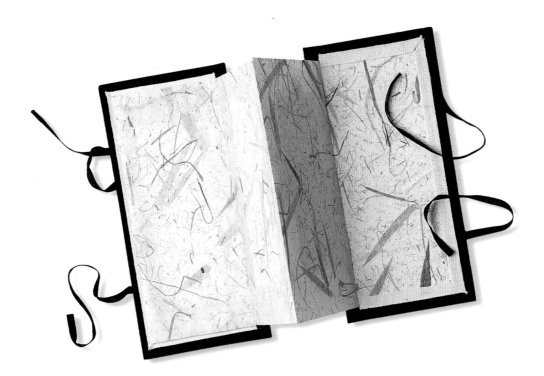